The PLANT GROWTH PLANNER

The PLANT GROWTH PLANNER

Two Hundred Illustrated Charts for
Shrubs, Trees, Climbers and Perennials

CAROLINE BOISSET

A **Horticulture** Book

PRENTICE HALL

New York London Toronto Sydney Tokyo Singapore

The Plant Growth Planner
Caroline Boisset

To Peter Thoday, Tom Wright, Elspeth Napier and
Robert Saxton who have given me encouragement
and unfailing support over many years.

 Prentice Hall General Reference
15 Columbus Circle
New York, New York 10023

Copyright © 1992 Mitchell Beazley Publishers
Text copyright © 1992 Caroline Boisset
Illustrations copyright © 1992 Mitchell Beazley
Publishers

Published by Mitchell Beazley International Ltd

PRENTICE HALL and colophon are registered
trademarks of Simon & Schuster, Inc.

A Horticulture Book
An Affiliate of *Horticulture*, The Magazine of
American Gardening

Library of Congress Cataloging-in-Publication Data
Boisset, Caroline
    The plant growth planner / Caroline Boisset
        p.   cm.
    Includes index.
    ISBN 0-13-681230-9
    1. Gardening.   2. Plants, Cultivated.   3.
Growth (Plants)
    I. Title
    SB453.B613   1992   91-42866
    635—dc20   CIP

Edited and designed by Mitchell Beazley
International Ltd
Michelin House, 81 Fulham Road, London SW3 6RB

Senior Editor Sarah Polden
Senior Art Editor Eljay Crompton
Designer Geoff Fennell
Illustrations Fiona Bell Currie, Sarah Kensington
American Editor Fayal Greene

The publishers have made every effort to ensure that
all instructions given in this book are accurate and
safe, but they cannot accept liability for any
resulting injury, damage or loss to either person or
property whether direct or consequential and
howsoever arising. The author and publishers will
be grateful for any information which will assist
them in keeping future editions up to date.

Printed in the United States

10 9 8 7 6 5 4 3 2 1

First Prentice Hall Edition

Contents

Right: The blue Himalayan poppy, *Meconopsis betonicifolia*, requires cool, moist summer conditions and good drainage to thrive, which makes it a difficult subject to grow in many areas. If conditions are favorable it can reach 4ft (1.2m) and will spread 1½ft (45cm).

Left: Herbaceous plants quickly develop into bold clumps in a border, making them a rewarding group of plants. If they are planted in a soil that is free of perennial weeds, they will be able to establish themselves well and will then suppress annual weeds. The most vigorous species need lifting and splitting in the autumn or spring to prevent them from smothering less robust plants. Here *Oenothera*, *Delphinium*, *Sedum*, *Geranium*, *Lupinus* and *Chrysanthemum* are combined to stunning effect.

Introduction

The purpose of this book is to facilitate the planned growth of a garden from youth to maturity. A garden with healthy, well-proportioned plants is every keen gardener's ambition. Most people, however, find it difficult to predict the speed with which they will grow over the years. No two plants are identical: environmental influences and varying methods of cultivation can produce different growth rates, even in plants vegetatively propagated from the same parent. However, given reasonably good soil, similar climatic conditions and accepted horticultural practice, plants of the same species will usually grow to approximately the same height by maturity. The charts included in this book give a good idea of the rates of growth achieved by particular plants in suitable conditions, but they are not definitive. They also present a very useful way of comparing growth from one species to another; fast-, medium- and slow-growers can be identified at a glance.

It is important that the gardener has a clear and realistic idea of how much time is available to manage the garden before selecting varieties to plant. This is very much a question of balancing speed of growth against maintenance. Fast-growing species require regular pruning and training, while slow-growing plants need much less maintenance but take longer to fulfil their promise. An alternative is to combine fast- and slow-growers, planting the former as a short-term covering, to be removed once the permanent scheme is established. This book includes a wealth of planting alternatives that enable the choice between speed and maintenance to be made.

The factors that influence plant growth are outlined in this introduction. This knowledge will assist the reader in interpreting the growth charts.

ENVIRONMENTAL FACTORS
Soil

Most plants grow best in moisture-retentive, well-drained, slightly acid to neutral soil. The perfect garden soil is a balance between humus, or well-rotted organic material (which retain moisture), and large mineral particles (which trap air and ensure good drainage). It must also contain the nutrients necessary for plant growth. The three main

nutrients are nitrogen, phosporus and potassium, supplemented by calcium, magnesium and sulphur. In addition there are the trace elements, iron, copper, boron, zinc, manganese and molybdenum, which are needed in very small quantities. Should any of these be deficient, the plant's photosynthesis mechanism will be impaired and growth will slow down or even stop.

It is often possible to improve the composition of a soil, whether structurally – by incorporating garden com-

This garden corner is a triumph of good planning and excellent care. The main focus among a wealth of species is the *Buddleia alternifolia*. This always makes a feature in a mixed border when in full-flower, but here the impact is accentuated by the fact that the plant has been trained as a standard. To do this a central stem should be selected and staked to keep it straight. It has to be pruned of any side shoots until the desired height is reached, at which point stems are allowed to grow out, forming a powder-puff shape. Unlike *B. davidii* which flowers on the current year's wood and is pruned in early spring, *B. alternifolia* flowers on the previous year's wood and should be pruned straight after flowering.

post, leaf mold, well-rotted farmyard manure or peat – or chemically – by adding specific nutrients or proprietary fertilizers. Goodness is constantly being taken out of the soil by growing plants and this must be replaced to maintain the balance.

The pH of the soil, the degree of acidity or alkalinity, is more difficult to alter significantly and can influence the choice of plants grown in the garden. Soils which have a pH below 7 are acid. Under 5.5 most plants will fail to grow,

leaving only heathers, moorland plants, rhododendrons and a few other species to flourish. Hydrated lime or ground chalk, applied in the winter, will reduce acidity slightly. Alkaline soils have a pH above 7. Heathers, rhododendrons, pieris, kalmias, lupines and lilies will not grow in these soils. Peat is most effective in reducing the pH of a soil, but, in the name of conservation, it is advisable not to use it in large quantities. Well-rotted manure, leaf mold or garden compost will slowly have an effect.

Penstemons are a large group of herbaceous plants that range in color from clear blue through red and pink to white. They vary in hardiness (the wider-leaved forms being most tender) but all species can easily be overwintered as cuttings taken in late summer. Here the cultivar 'Garnet' is growing with the variegated *Cornus alba* 'Elegantissima'.

Climate

The climate of an area is the other main factor that dictates which plants can be grown and the rate at which they will grow.

TEMPERATURE The most important temperature to be considered in relation to plant growth is the degree of cold a species can tolerate. As an aid to the North American horticultural industry, the Arnold Arboretum of Harvard

University compiled a map of plant hardiness zones, each numbered zone denoting a range of average annual minimum temperatures. Another map has been devised along the same lines for Europe (see p. 12-13).

Summer heat, too, can influence growth rates. In North America certain introduced species such as ampelopsis and the Norway maple may become invasive, given the hot sun and the right soil. Others such as night-scented stock go dormant in summer's intense heat. The wide range of climates, from arctic to tropical, allows virtually every plant to be grown somewhere in the United States and Canada: the fact that plants from widely-differing zones can be grown together in the temperate British climate is to be envied.

PRECIPITATION The total amount of precipitation in a year, be it snow, rain or hail, in combination with the retentive or draining qualities of the soil, will affect plant growth enormously. The smaller the plant, the less water it will require – but the sooner it will wilt if deprived of water. Some plants, particularly bulbous species and annuals, have evolved to survive long periods of drought. Once it has rained they flower and seed very quickly, completing their life cycle while conditions are favorable. Some 30in (75cm) of rain a year is sufficient for most trees but any shortfall will only be apparent after a lapse of two or three years.

The timing of rainfall is a crucial factor. The specific needs of every plant are dictated by its pattern of growth. For example, if a period of drought ends in late spring, it will happily coincide with the beginning of a yew's growing season, but it may have come too late to save a beech, which will have revived from dormancy earlier in the season and could have expended its limited energies on early growth.

WIND Plants regularly exposed to strong winds can be stunted or may even fail. High winds combined with dry, crumbly soil present a most inhospitable environment for garden plants. By improving the soil with plenty of humus-rich material and erecting an artificial windbreak, many plants can be established. Wind-tolerant, fast-growing species such as pines, buckthorn, alder, poplars, birch and some cypresses, will provide a useful sheltered belt for more susceptible varieties. Solid walls may cause the wind to eddy and damage the garden more extensively.

MICROCLIMATES The amount of sun and wind a garden receives largely depends on its situation and contours: whether it is flat or sloping, stands on high or low ground, is warm and south-facing or a frost-pocket. In this way, a garden can have a microclimate that differs from the general climate of the region. One part of a garden can have a different microclimate from another. It is worth trying plants that are considered

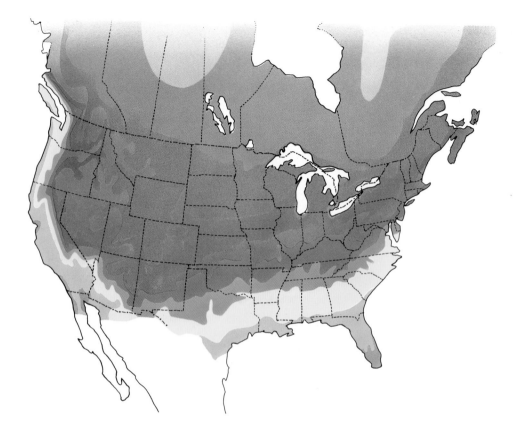

tender for the area in sheltered corners or against a wall. Equally, particularly exposed sites should be given additional protection from cold and wind.

SALT AND POLLUTION These environmental factors, one natural to coastal areas, the other man-made, affect plants to varying degrees. A screen made from resistant species can considerably reduce the damage done to vulnerable plants.

CULTIVATION
Moisture, light and a sufficiently high temperature are the three environmental essentials that govern the growth of plants. If even one of these is in short supply growth will slow down or possibly stop. The aim of good horticultural practice is to ensure that all the essentials are available to garden plants at the right time.

When to plant
The best time to plant species is during their dormant period. For most bulbs this is during autumn, for evergreens it is in early to mid-autumn or mid- to late spring, and for deciduous woody species

ZONES OF HARDINESS
These maps show zones of
average annual minimum
temperatures. The zone
numbers are used to indicate
plant hardiness.

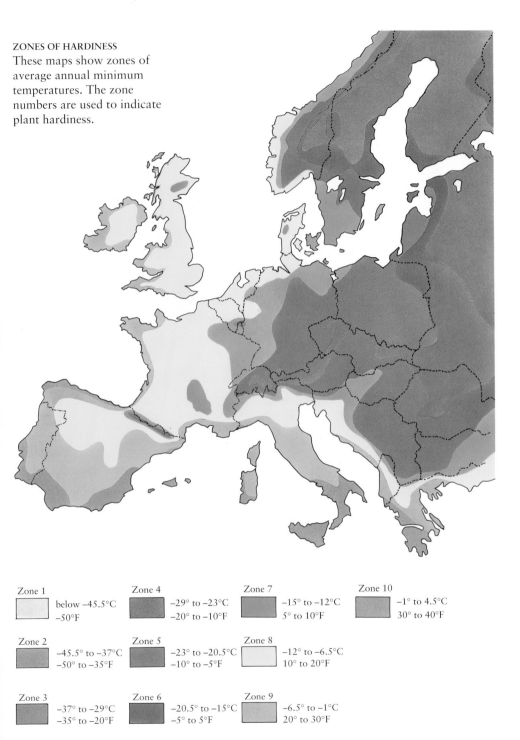

Zone 1		below −45.5°C −50°F
Zone 2		−45.5° to −37°C −50° to −35°F
Zone 3		−37° to −29°C −35° to −20°F

Zone 4		−29° to −23°C −20° to −10°F
Zone 5		−23° to −20.5°C −10° to −5°F
Zone 6		−20.5° to −15°C −5° to 5°F

Zone 7		−15° to −12°C 5° to 10°F
Zone 8		−12° to −6.5°C 10° to 20°F
Zone 9		−6.5° to −1°C 20° to 30°F

| Zone 10 | | −1° to 4.5°C 30° to 40°F |

and herbaceous perennials it is in spring, providing the conditions are right; that is, the soil is not waterlogged and the temperature is not too high. If conditions are unsuitable, new planting should be delayed until autumn.

In practice, planting tends to be done either at the end of autumn, when growth has nearly stopped but the soil is still warm, or, more usually, at the beginning of spring, just before growth starts and the soil is warming up. Which season is better largely depends on the climate. Where winters are severe, plant in spring; where the climate is milder, autumn is better as this tends to be a wetter season. Containerized plants can be planted throughout the growing season. Whatever the time of year, young plants will need regular watering to become established.

Watering and nutrients

In early spring a dose of a good slow-release NPK (nitrogen, phosphorus and potassium) fertilizer should be applied around all plants, to supplement the nutrients in the soil. Manure and compost will also add nutrients. Spring is the most important time to ensure that enough moisture is available. It is better to water copiously at longer intervals than little and often. To check if plants have received sufficient water, dig into the soil with a stick an hour or so after watering and see how deep the moisture goes. The water should have

This large mixed border is shown in early spring when the hellebores and daffodils are coming into flower. Peonies, irises and delphiniums are emerging and will take center stage in late spring and early summer. Later still there will be a sea of phlox. A substantial layer of mulch was spread over the ground to suppress weeds, conserve moisture and increase the nutrient content of the soil.

Once an ornamental plant is established, except in extraordinary circumstances, it should require very little watering other than during the spring. If it does, then the climate or soil is not suitable and it will always be difficult to grow satisfactorily.

Preparation for winter
It is important to make sure that the soil is not too wet at the onset of winter. Excess water will freeze around the roots of the plant and can destroy the plant cells – which highlights the benefit of a sharply-draining soil. A plant that has a high water content is much more likely to rot and die during its inactive phase than one that has endured a dry period, so refrain from watering your garden as autumn draws to a close.

Some woody species require a long growing season before they can withstand a bad winter; if their wood is only partially ripe they may succumb to a fairly mild one. This can be forestalled by applying potash around the roots in mid- to late summer, thereby causing the new growth to ripen.

penetrated at least 3 or 4in (7.5-10cm) for herbaceous perennials, in excess of 6in (15cm) for young shrubs, and over 1ft (30cm) for trees. As a rough rule, the water should penetrate as deeply as the roots of the plant to be most effective (probing tree-roots are an obvious exception to these guidelines).

If water is scarce, an upright plastic bottle with a pinprick in the base can be buried to the appropriate depth near a plant. This can be filled with water, thereby ensuring that moisture goes directly to the roots without wastage.

Pruning
Pruning has several aims: the first is to train plants into shape by building a sound framework or to restrict plants that grow beyond their boundaries; the second is to encourage vigorous young growth and maximum flowering, either

in the same or the subsequent year; a third is to remove dead or diseased branches.

It is worth investing in quality implements, looking after them and keeping them sharp. The essential tools are a good pair of pruners, a small pruning saw and long-handled lopping shears.

A clean cut is always better than a jagged tear as the latter increases the chances of disease entering the wound. Make the cut about ¼in (5mm) above the bud, which should be plump and healthy and pointing in the direction in which a new shoot is required to grow.

Generally speaking, a plant that is pruned hard will grow back most vigorously. It therefore follows that a shrub that is growing more strongly on one side than the other should be most severely pruned on the weak side, while it is dormant, to encourage plenty of new growth. The other side should be left until the second half of the growing season, when pruning will curtail growth. The plant will be in full leaf so

Right: Trees can have radically different habits. The rounded head of *Gleditsia triacanthos* 'Sunburst' bears feathery foliage in spring and contrasts with the gaunt upright silhouette of an Irish yew, *Taxus baccata* 'Fastigiata'.
Far right: The correct way to prune any stem is to make a sloping cut away from the selected bud, about ¼in (5mm) above it. Any higher leaves a stem that is prone to die back and could become a seat for disease. A cut that is too low may damage the bud.

it can easily be shaped for balance. This is also a good time to cut out any dead wood which can be difficult to distinguish from dormant wood in winter.

Most shrubs and climbers require little or no pruning other than the removal of dead, weak or diseased stems and slight trimming to maintain balanced growth. This rule also applies to trees in their formative years. Dead-heading can extend the flowering season and neatens the plant, but it is not always essential and, indeed, can be counterproductive; for example, unless great care is used when dead-heading rhododendrons, the following season's flowers, which form just below the existing flowers, can be damaged.

Some shrubs and climbers *do* need

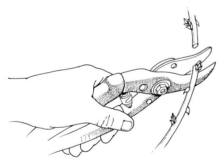

regular pruning at particular times of year if they are to produce quantities of blossoms and well-colored foliage. Those that bear flowers on the current year's growth should be pruned back in late winter or early spring. Some, such as *Buddleia davidii* (butterfly bush), large-flowered clematis and *Caryopteris*, can be cut down to near ground level.

Other plants, such as *Campsis radicans* (trumpet vine), eccremocarpus and deciduous ceanothus species, should only be pruned back to a strong young bud.

Shrubs and climbers that flower on the previous year's shoots should be pruned soon after flowering in late spring or early summer. This will allow young shoots maximum time to grow up and flower the following year. These plants include philadelphus species, *Clematis montana* and forsythias.

Shrubs that are grown for their decorative winter bark or foliage need to be pruned hard back in the spring to encourage the growth of strong young shoots. *Cornus alba* (red-barked dogwood), *Salix alba* (white willow) and *Cotinus coggygria* 'Notcutt's Variety' are examples of such plants.

Evergreen climbers should be sheared over in the spring to remove old, tatty leaves and to promote the growth of fresh leaves.

The pruning of formal hedges is, in the main, dictated by their growth rates. Fast-growing species should be pruned for control during the growing season, slow-growers should be pruned during the dormant season to encourage growth. Informal hedges can be treated like shrubs and pruned to improve flowering or leaf growth.

THE GROWTH CHARTS

These are divided into six sections: trees, shrubs, climbers, ground cover, herbaceous perennials and hedges.

With the exception of herbaceous perennials, the plants in each group are listed alphabetically. As herbaceous perennials are rarely used in isolation, these have been grouped according to size and color, to give some suggestions of plant associations. Heights are indicated on the charts by means of a grid; plan views of ground cover and herbaceous perennials show the likely spread of these plants.

For every example, three or four growth stages are represented, each at a different season, thereby showing how the plant changes through the year as well as over a longer span of time. The amount of growth illustrated assumes correct, sufficient pruning has been undertaken where relevant. The period of 12 years has been chosen for trees, shrubs and climbers, as by this time trees have reached a recognizable form and shrubs and climbers are at their peak. Eight-years' growth is shown for hedges, because a reasonable barrier should have been achieved by this time, and three for ground cover plants, at which point they should provide good weed control. Herbaceous perennials

grow up every year to the same height, but they spread annually and usually need lifting and dividing after about three years, so this is the period illustrated in the growth charts.

Each plant charted in the book also has a descriptive entry. The botanical name is always given and the common name and synonyms where relevant. The plant's characteristics are standard details, as are sizes that would be achieved under optimum conditions, but only essential soil requirements are included; where no mention is made of soils it should be assumed that an aver-

age to good neutral soil (between pH 6 and 7) is suitable for the plant. In most cases a few (but by no means all) cultivars or hybrids are mentioned as alternatives; these are indicated in a bold typeface. Hardiness zones (see p. 10-13) are given for each plant, as well as the suitable light intensity (full sun or shade; if alternatives are given, the preferred degree of light is stated first). The ultimate height and sometimes spread a single plant can be expected to achieve are given (denoted by u.h. and u.s.).

The entries for shrubs, climbers and hedges include advice on pruning, indicated by a series of codes:

▲: a plant that requires little or no pruning other than dead-heading, shaping, curtailing and the removal of dead or diseased material.

■: a plant that bears flowers on the current year's shoots: prune hard back in late winter or early spring.

●: a plant that bears flowers on the previous year's shoots: prune soon after flowering ends.

◆: a plant that has striking winter bark or foliage: prune hard back in spring.

✳: a hedge or climber: prune in winter.

◗: an evergreen hedge: prune in spring.

✚: a foliage hedge: prune in summer.

❖: a hedge: prune in late summer.

Some hedges have alternative pruning periods (indicated by an oblique stroke between the codes), others need to be pruned more than once a year, shown by a pair of codes.

Herbaceous borders lead to a beech hedge which in turn directs the eye to tall Leyland cypresses beyond. In summer (left) the abundant white blooms and rich display of foliage are most striking; in autumn (above) it is the range of heights and masses that give interest.

Right: The upright habit of this mountain ash or rowan, *Sorbus aucuparia*, is set off by the delicate foliage. This tree grows rapidly to 20ft (6m) or more in 20 years. The flowers are succeeded by berries that ripen in summer, and the foliage assumes warm orange tints in autumn.

Trees

Left: A pink form of the dogwood, *Cornus florida*, a striking multi-stemmed small tree, sometimes classified as a large shrub as it rarely reaches more than 20ft (6m). The flowers are followed in warm climates by small red berries and the foliage turns red and purple in autumn.

Choosing the right tree for the right place in a garden can be a daunting prospect. Many trees take a long time to make a significant impact and then, when they do, they have often reached sizes that are out of all proportion with the house or the garden. This is all the more serious in small gardens where space and light are at a premium. But the range of trees worth growing is so vast, there is sure to be one to suit any situation, even if it requires pruning. There are fast-growing trees and much slower-growing trees, and many which, even at maturity, remain medium or small in size. Trees have much to recommend them and fulfil such an important role in the garden that the presence of one or two in even the tiniest space is to be encouraged.

Of all garden plants, trees are the longest-lived, and as they mature they impart a valuable air of timelessness to their surroundings. They are the most effective plants for enforcing the vertical dimension of a garden; their stature gives solidity to a planting scheme. Trees can also provide shade and protection from frost and wind for other plants and for people.

The qualities that make individual trees worth growing are: beauty of form and habit; attractive foliage, whether in color, shape or texture; striking flowers and fruit; handsome bark or highly colored twigs.

The illustrations in this section show the rates of growth that are possible in the first 12 years after planting. The ultimate height for each example is included at the end of the corresponding entry, and it is important that this is noted. A little over half of the trees included are relatively small; that is, they rarely reach more than 50ft (15m)

Far left: Japanese flowering cherries are medium sized trees that are covered in blossom in spring. The leaves that follow are most beautiful in autumn and the highly polished bark glistens in winter.

Left: A beautiful example of the weeping willow-leaved pear, *Pyrus salicifolia* 'Pendula', the white flowers mingling with the silvery spring foliage.

in height. These include the flowering cherry *Prunus serrulata*, the saucer magnolia (*Magnolia × soulangiana*), the paperbark maple (*Acer griseum*) and the Persian iron tree (*Parrotia persica*). There are a few very small trees (although no dwarfs) that are under 20ft (6m) at maturity; for example, the English hawthorn (*Crataegus laevigata*) and the weeping willow-leaved pear (*Pyrus salicifolia* 'Pendula'). The remainder rank among the giants of our woodlands, for the most part exceeding 100ft (30m). The English oak (*Quercus robur*), dawn redwood (*Metasequoia glyptostroboides* and Scotch pine (*Pinus sylvestris*) come into this category. Speed of growth varies enormously from one species to another, even if their ultimate height is the same. For example, both the paper bark birch (*Betula papyrifera*) and the dove tree (*Davidia involucrata*) can be expected to reach some 60ft (18m) at maturity, but the former will have achieved a

good 40ft (12m) in 20 years, while the latter will only be 15ft (4.5m) tall in the same period.

The size of a mature tree is the single most important factor that must be considered when selecting a species for a given space. The handsome maidenhair tree (*Ginkgo biloba*) will reach only about 20ft (6m) in 20 years but it could easily achieve 80ft (24m) or more at maturity. An average town garden would eventually be swamped by such an unsuitable species, and the tree's very removal could cause the gardener great difficulties.

Another consideration, aesthetic as well as practical, is the shape of a tree. Trees with a rounded leaf canopy are a pleasing sight, but they can require a good deal of space and may cast large shadows. A columnar specimen – one which has close-growing vertical branches – will be best for a narrow space. This shape is often denoted by 'Fastigiata' or 'Columnaris' in cultivar names, for example *Acer platanoides* 'Columnare' and *Taxus baccata* 'Fastigiata'. Weeping trees often include the words *pendula* or 'weeping' in their name, such as *Betula pendula* 'Youngii' and *Prunus* 'Cheal's Weeping'. Pyramidal-shaped trees are yet another alternative.

Choosing the best place for a tree is an important decision. The shade the tree casts may, in time, become detrimental to the garden; alternatively, it may provide very welcome protection from the hottest sun in the middle of the day. Tall trees can form an excellent windbreak, although they can also block a fine view. In a larger space a small tree can be used as a focal point for the whole or part of the garden, forming the nucleus of a complementary planting design. Such a specimen will cast a pleasing, rotating shadow on sunny days. In a small space a tree is best planted on the boundary where it will not cause excessive shade, provided that it is not too near a building.

There is no unanimous view on the distance to allow between a building and the site of a new tree. Tree roots can certainly cause serious damage to buildings, to their foundations and drains, and some authorities suggest that a tree should be no closer to a house than its height at maturity. But I have often seen trees nearly 100ft (30m) tall and a century or more old that are within 30ft (9m) of a building, without

any report of damage to the structure. In a large open space such trees are a foil to a house, while in townscapes their value can never be overstated. The most frequently heard objection to large trees is the way they cut out light from a house; another, more serious complaint is that a severe winter gale may bring a tree down onto a building.

The species of the tree and the nature of the soil and the site are important factors in determining the threat posed by a tree to a building. For example, willows are renowned for their long, questing roots which can do considerable damage to drains. Shallow-rooted trees, which include many pines, should not be planted on light soil in exposed

positions as there is a good chance that they could be blown over. A knowledge of your tree and your site has to be combined with common sense: it will benefit neither the tree nor a house to plant a sapling very close to structural walls. Pruning can go some way in containing a tree, but if a mistake has clearly been made in positioning the tree, cut it down before it becomes a menace.

The decision to have a mature tree felled must be taken only after careful thought, particularly in an urban context where its presence makes an important contribution to the environment, beyond the immediate confines of the garden. There may also be legal

Left: This multi-stemmed pine has a windswept appearance, characteristic of so many pine species. Its wide canopy casts a shadow over a collection of shade-tolerant shrubs. The tree is in proportion with the house, complementing the structure.

Above: Crab apples are among the largest group of medium sized ornamental fruiting trees. Here is *Malus* 'Golden Hornet', which reaches 15 to 20ft (4.5-6m) in 20 years.

restrictions on the removal of trees; investigate this possibility before taking action or there could be a fine to pay.

Creating excessive shade has doomed many mature trees. As an alternative to execution, use the cover as an asset and make a woodland garden of shade-loving plants under deciduous trees, or a spring garden of species that flower before the leaf canopy is full. It is also possible, with the services of a specialist tree surgeon, to thin the canopy of a tree drastically without altering its visual impact. This will make the shaded area hospitable to more garden species.

If a large tree dies it may be tempting to grow a vigorous climber through it. But a dead stump is a seat for honey fungus, a serious and destructive plant disease. In addition, the space taken up by the stump could probably be better used. Either cut the tree to the ground and treat the stump with stump remover or call in a qualified arboriculturist who will remove the roots as well. The last option is expensive and disruptive in the short term, but it allows for a fresh start in ground freed of an extensive root system.

If you choose to replace an old tree with a new one, consider buying a fairly mature specimen, described as an "extra heavy standard" in the nursery trade; that is, a tree upwards of 10ft (3m) tall with a trunk girth of 12 to 20in (30-50cm). Such a tree will make an immediate impact on the garden. A

disadvantage is that it may take a few years to settle and make new growth (some three to five years), unlike a younger plant which will have put on significant growth by the second year. Extra heavy standards are also much more expensive than younger trees.

Whether it is a large or small tree, remember to plant it in a hole large enough to accommodate its existing roots comfortably. Incorporate organic matter and some slow-release fertilizer when filling the hole. A short stake, treated against rot, driven firmly into the base of the planting pit, will provide stability while the tree becomes established. The stake need only extend a

quarter or a third of the height of the tree and can be taken out after two or three years. Attach the tree securely to the stake with a good-quality tie, making it neither too tight nor too slack. Check the bond from time to time, in case it has broken or is injuring the tree.

A regular pruning routine is advisable in the early years of a tree's life to ensure that it grows into a shapely specimen. Crossing branches should be removed, along with dead or diseased ones. Rub out any shoots on the trunk to prevent low branches from developing. A few species can be pruned hard back to encourage particular attributes: lindens and willows, to produce colorful twigs; paulownias and ailanthuses, to develop enormous leaves.

Left: Trees with contrasting or complementary foliage and habits can be combined very effectively if space permits. Here, a dwarf conifer and a purple *Mahonia aquifolium* have been coupled, with a young specimen of the Serbian spruce, *Picea omorika*, behind. This spruce develops a pendulous habit with upward turning branches. It is very hardy and reaches 10ft (3m) in ten years. Above: Many trees have striking bark that stands out in the winter. The silver birch, *Betula pendula*, is a fast-growing species that reaches over 30ft (10m). The peeling bark only appears as the tree matures, after seven to ten years.

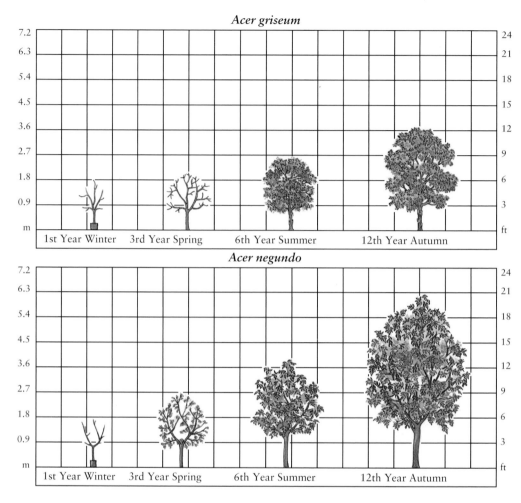

Acer griseum

7.2 / 24
6.3 / 21
5.4 / 18
4.5 / 15
3.6 / 12
2.7 / 9
1.8 / 6
0.9 / 3
m / ft

1st Year Winter   3rd Year Spring   6th Year Summer   12th Year Autumn

Acer negundo

7.2 / 24
6.3 / 21
5.4 / 18
4.5 / 15
3.6 / 12
2.7 / 9
1.8 / 6
0.9 / 3
m / ft

1st Year Winter   3rd Year Spring   6th Year Summer   12th Year Autumn

Acer griseum

Paperbark maple

A tree for all seasons that grows steadily, reaching some 20ft (6m) in 20 years, and, unlike most maples, it is tolerant of alkaline soils. This most attractive tree has beautiful orangey-brown peeling bark which gives it immense appeal in winter. The deciduous trifoliate leaves, with a span of approximately 2 to 4in (5-10cm), open late. At first a dark shade of yellow-buff, they turn dark green in summer and deep scarlet and red in autumn. The flowers are greenish-yellow when they open in early summer.

z 4-8 sun u.h. 40ft (12m)

Acer negundo

Box elder

A very fast-growing deciduous tree, reaching nearly 30ft (9m) in 20 years. It has pinnate leaves up to 8in (20cm) long which have earned it the alternative name of ash-leaved maple. The dioecious flowers hang in long racemes and open mid-spring, before the leaves appear. **'Flamingo'** is the most attractive and least vigorous variegated form. This reaches 10ft (3m) or a little more, with leaves that turn from light pink to green with white and pinkish markings. **'Auratum'** has bright golden yellow leaves.

z 4-8 partial shade u.h. 45 ft (14m)

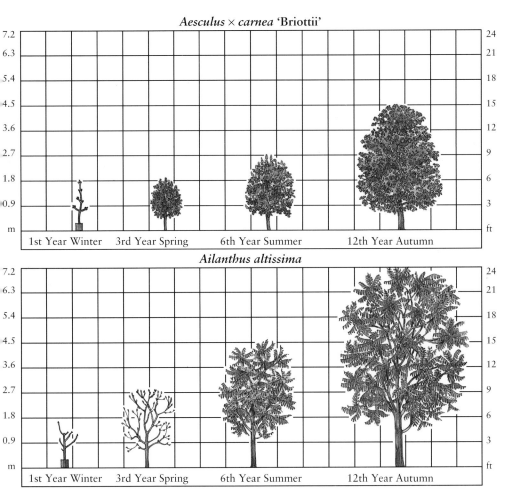

Aesculus × carnea 'Briottii'

1st Year Winter   3rd Year Spring   6th Year Summer   12th Year Autumn

Ailanthus altissima

1st Year Winter   3rd Year Spring   6th Year Summer   12th Year Autumn

Aesculus × carnea 'Briottii'

Red horse chestnut

Although more compact and smaller than the common horse chestnut, this deciduous tree is suitable only for large gardens as it will reach 20ft (6m) in 20 years, with an oval canopy. The digitate leaves are up to 1ft (30cm) across and are smoother and darker green than the common form; in autumn they turn a deep orangey-yellow. Upright panicles, 10in (25cm) long, bear deep red flowers. The "conkers" are smooth-coated. Like most horse chestnuts it dislikes a very limy soil and requires plenty of moisture.

z 5-7 sun or partial shade u.h. 40ft (12m)

Ailanthus altissima

Tree of heaven

This is one of the most vigorous and fastest growing trees, reaching 45ft (14m) in 20 years. In some areas it is considered a weed. The deciduous canopy is light and somewhat irregular with leaves that resemble those of an ash but are much larger at 1 to 2ft (30-60cm) long; they are yellow in the autumn. The small panicles of yellow-green flowers appear in late summer to early autumn, followed by winged greeny-crimson fruit. If cut down each spring it makes a tropical-looking plant with leaves up to 4ft (1.2m) long.

z 4-8 sun or partial shade u.h. 80ft (24m)

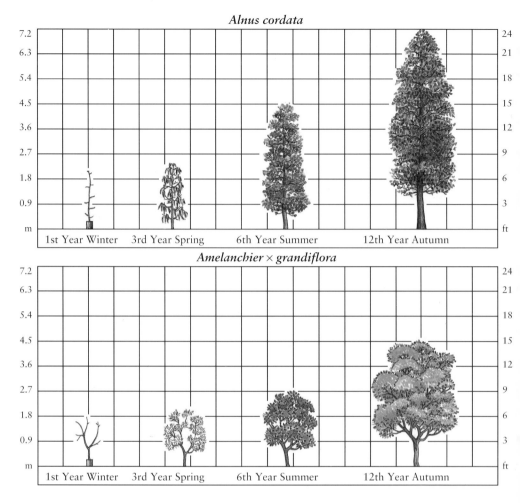

Alnus cordata

7.2										24
6.3										21
5.4										18
4.5										15
3.6										12
2.7										9
1.8										6
0.9										3
m	1st Year Winter	3rd Year Spring	6th Year Summer	12th Year Autumn						ft

Amelanchier × grandiflora

7.2										24
6.3										21
5.4										18
4.5										15
3.6										12
2.7										9
1.8										6
0.9										3
m	1st Year Winter	3rd Year Spring	6th Year Summer	12th Year Autumn						ft

Alnus cordata

Italian alder

An easy-to-grow deciduous tree, of a
distinctively tall, narrow conical shape,
which reaches 40ft (12m) in 20 years. The
crown is adorned with catkins in the early
spring. These turn into little round fruits
in the autumn which persist throughout
the winter. The leaves are a shiny dark
green on top and lighter underneath. This
alder will grow in any soil, dry or damp,
acid or alkaline. For particularly boggy
ground the common alder, **A. glutinosa**,
is better, while the grey alder, **A. incana**,
is best for poor, reclaimed soils.

z 4-7 sun or partial shade u.h. 80ft (24m)

Amelanchier × grandiflora

Shadbush or serviceberry

This small deciduous tree, also known as
A. lamarckii, has a low rounded canopy
and is often grown as a multi-stemmed
shrub, reaching 20ft (6m) or so in 20
years. The delicate white flowers appear
in early spring as the soft coppery leaves
are unfurling. The leaves turn to green
through the summer and form a
background to the crimson fruit. In early
autumn the fruit ripens to black and the
leaves turn orange or red. It does best in
moist soils and dislikes alkalinity.

z 4-7 partial shade u.h. 30ft (9m)

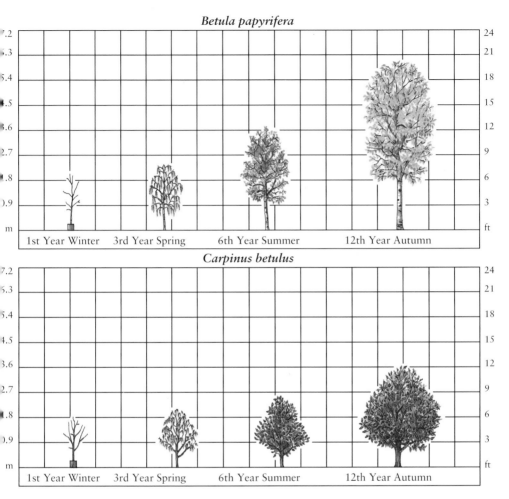

Betula papyrifera

Paper birch or canoe birch

This deciduous tree rapidly reaches nearly 40ft (12m) in 20 years. Its open canopy casts only partial shade. The tree's chief attraction is the smooth white bark which persists throughout the year. This develops during the first five years after planting and peels off in great sheets, revealing glistening new layers beneath. The irregularly toothed small leaves turn yellow in autumn. **B. pendula 'Tristis'** is the weeping form which grows to 33ft (10m) in 20 years and has graceful pendulous branches.

z 2-7 sun or shade u.h. 60ft (18m)

Carpinus betulus

Common hornbeam

This deciduous tree responds well to frequent pruning. Traditionally pollarded in Europe, it is also suitable for hedging (see **Fagus sylvatica**, p.170). When grown as a specimen, it makes a smaller tree than beech, reaching 26ft (8m) in 20 years. The narrow, early growth slowly spreads out into a wide, rounded canopy. The toothed leaves open early and are bright green in summer, turning yellow and brown in autumn. It grows well in most soils, particularly heavy, damp ones where beech fails.

z 4-8 sun or shade u.h. 60ft (18m)

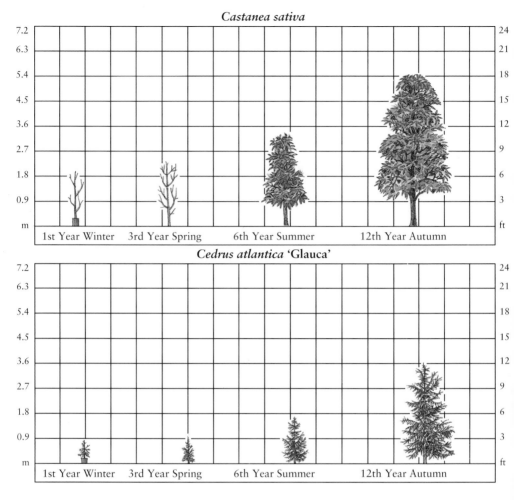

Castanea sativa

Spanish chestnut

A fine deciduous tree for a large garden, reaching 40ft (12m) in 20 years. Its narrow crown broadens out as the tree matures and the grey bark assumes its characteristic spiralling grooves. The bright green, toothed leaves are up to 10in (25cm) long; they turn rusty in the autumn. Greeny-yellow tasseled catkins appear in mid-summer and are followed by shiny edible fruits, two or three in each prickly shell. It thrives in sharply draining sandy soil. The smaller Chinese chestnut, *C. mollissima,* is less susceptible to blight.

z 6-9 sun or partial shade u.h. 100ft (30m)

Cedrus atlantica 'Glauca'

Atlas cedar

The Atlas cedar is second only to its cousin the Lebanese cedar (*C. libani*) in beauty and stature but is hardier and easier to grow. The blue-gray form of this evergreen conifer is most commonly found in cultivation and has a pyramidal shape when young with upward growing branches reaching barely 20ft (6m) in 20 years. Eventually it assumes the flat-topped shape typical of all cedars. The pendulous form, *C. atlantica* 'Glauca Pendula', grows to about 33ft (10m) with hanging branches and leaders.

z 6-9 sun u.h. 110ft (33m)

Cercidiphyllum japonicum

7.2			24
6.3			21
5.4			18
4.5			15
3.6			12
2.7			9
1.8			6
0.9			3
m			ft

| 1st Year Winter | 3rd Year Spring | 6th Year Summer | 12th Year Autumn |

Crataegus laevigata 'Crimson Cloud'

7.2			24
6.3			21
5.4			18
4.5			15
3.6			12
2.7			9
1.8			6
0.9			3
m			ft

| 1st Year Winter | 3rd Year Spring | 6th Year Summer | 12th Year Autumn |

Cercidiphyllum japonicum

Katsura tree
In the wild this tree grows to a staggering 100ft (30m) or more but in cultivation it achieves 23ft (7m) in 20 years. It has a broad oval-shaped crown of rounded to heart-shaped leaves. These open orangey-pink and turn sea-green above and bluish beneath. In autumn they turn a marvelous mixture of grayish-pink, vermilion and yellow and exude a rich smell of burning caramel. The tiny flowers that appear before the leaves are followed by 1in (2.5cm) long seed pods.

z 5-9 sun or partial shade u.h. 60ft (18m)

Crataegus laevigata 'Crimson Cloud'

Also classified as C. oxyacantha, the English hawthorn grows to about 10ft (3m) in ten years. 'Crimson Cloud' has glossy green deciduous leaves and clusters of large, deep red flowers with white patches at the base of each petal. In autumn a plentiful crop of shiny red berries lasts for at least six weeks. **'Paul's Scarlet'** is a commonly grown cultivar with quantities of deep pink double flowers in early summer and autumn fruits. The most hardy form is **'Toba'** which has double white flowers that turn pink as they age and later bright red fruit.

z 4-7 sun or shade u.h. 16ft (5m)

33

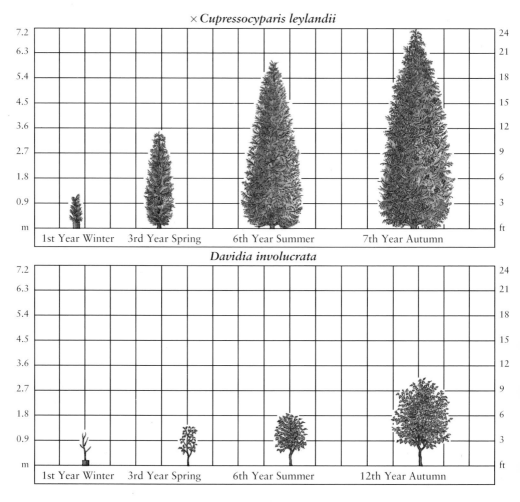

× *Cupressocyparis leylandii*

1st Year Winter   3rd Year Spring   6th Year Summer   7th Year Autumn

Davidia involucrata

1st Year Winter   3rd Year Spring   6th Year Summer   12th Year Autumn

× *Cupressocyparis leylandii*

Leyland cypress

In optimum conditions this tree is one of the fastest growing of all evergreen conifers and forms a good windbreak or makes a fine specimen in a large garden. It will reach 33ft (10m) in 12 years. For a screen or hedge, clip it early in growth: a large plant will be disfigured by severe pruning. A first-class screen at least 15ft (4.5m) high can be achieved in ten years. The gray-green foliage should be trimmed into shape in late spring and late summer, particularly in the early years of growth. 'Castlewellan' is a golden form.

z 6-9 sun or partial shade u.h. 100ft (30m)

Davidia involucrata

Dove, ghost or handkerchief tree

A rare but delightful plant, this is a slow grower, reaching 15ft (4.5m) in 20 years. It has a conical habit when young that becomes more rounded with age. The broad ovate leaves are a bright, fresh green above and a paler green below, but its chief glory is its extraordinary inflorescences. The female flower is surrounded by a mass of browny-purple male flowers which are protected by two white, paper-thin bracts 7in (17.5cm) long. These give the tree its common names. It requires a sheltered position.

z 6-8 sun u.h. 60ft (18m)

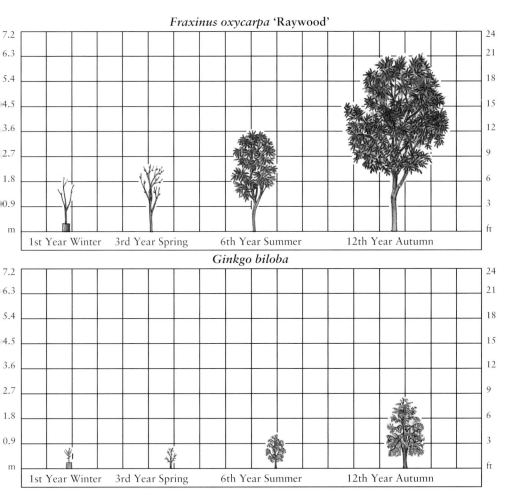

Fraxinus oxycarpa 'Raywood'

7.2												24
6.3												21
5.4												18
4.5												15
3.6												12
2.7												9
1.8												6
0.9												3
m												ft

1st Year Winter   3rd Year Spring   6th Year Summer   12th Year Autumn

Ginkgo biloba

1st Year Winter   3rd Year Spring   6th Year Summer   12th Year Autumn

Fraxinus oxycarpa 'Raywood'

Raywood ash
This ash rapidly makes a fine specimen tree reaching some 35ft (10.5m) in 20 years. The narrow canopy that broadens with age looks most striking when the deciduous pinnate leaves turn a reddy-purple in autumn. The petalless flowers are almost invisible. The manna ash, **F. ornus**, is much less vigorous, reaching only 16ft (5m) in 20 years. It bears quantities of panicles of dirty white flowers, which are fragrant in early summer. The autumn sees orangey-brown seed keys and purple foliage.

z 6-8 sun u.h. 65ft (19.5m)

Ginkgo biloba

Maidenhair tree
This deciduous conifer is the oldest surviving species in cultivation. It is slow to establish but grows quite steadily once settled and reaches about 20ft (6m) in 20 years. The leaves are fan-shaped with a central division, pale green in spring, yellow in autumn. Trees are single-sex. Female flowers are tiny; male flowers are 1in (2.5cm) catkins. The fruit resembles a hard yellow plum and smells of rancid butter when ripe, so it is best to grow male trees. The nut-like seed is edible. Ginkgo is resistant to pollution.

z 3-9 sun u.h. 80ft (24m)

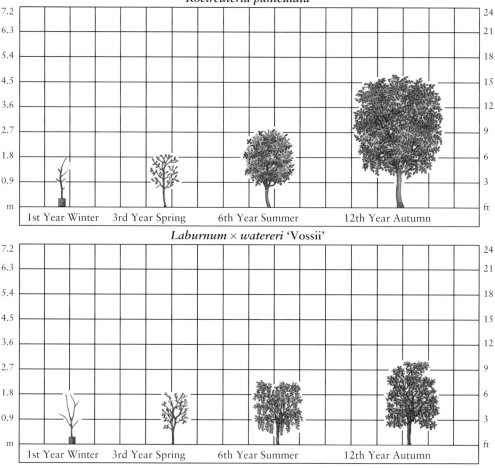

Koelreuteria paniculata

1st Year Winter   3rd Year Spring   6th Year Summer   12th Year Autumn

Laburnum × watereri 'Vossii'

1st Year Winter   3rd Year Spring   6th Year Summer   12th Year Autumn

Koelreuteria paniculata

Golden rain tree

Suitable as a specimen in a town garden, this tree grows to 20ft (6m) or more in 20 years. The pinnate (sometimes bipinnate) leaves with red petioles open pale yellow, turn dark green and then yellow again in the autumn. The small yellow flowers open in mid- to late summer in upright terminal panicles about 1ft (30cm) long. The bladder-like fruit is green at first, turning yellow and then brown in a good autumn. A hardy plant, it thrives in well-drained soil, withstands heat and drought, and tolerates alkalinity and pollution.

z 5-9 sun u.h. 30ft (9m)

Laburnum × watereri 'Vossii'

Golden chain tree

This is one of the best and most commonly grown forms of hybrid laburnum. Grown as a tree it reaches 15ft (4.5m) in 20 years but it can also be trained to make an attractive arch. It has 2ft (60cm) long racemes of deep yellow pea-flowers in early summer and leaves comprising three leaflets. This cultivar does not produce seed pods; on other forms these should be removed soon after blooming as they tend to reduce the vigour of the tree and are poisonous. It grows in any reasonably well-drained soil.

z 6-7 sun u.h. 25ft (7.5m)

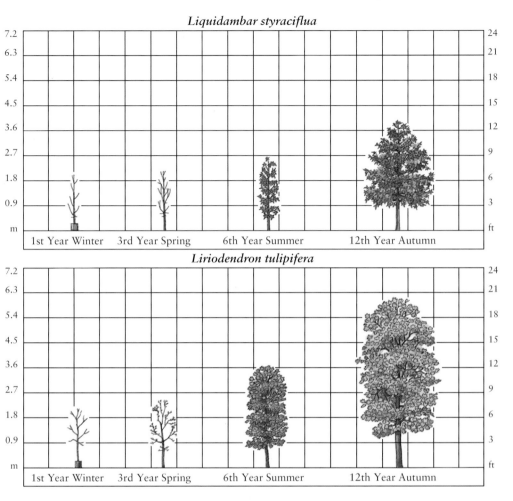

Liquidambar styraciflua

Sweet gum

This deciduous tree is a native of the eastern United States and does best in deep, moist, neutral to acid soil, reaching 15 to 20ft (4.5-6m) in 20 years. It develops a conical canopy of lobed, maple-like leaves that are deep green in summer and bright red with hints of purple, yellow and orange in the autumn. Of comparable beauty in the autumn and requiring similar conditions is the tupelo, *Nyssa sylvatica*, which is slightly smaller, with an ultimate height of 100ft (30m). The oval leaves turn orange and yellow.

z 6-9 sun or partial shade u.h. 150ft (45m)

Liriodendron tulipifera

Tulip tree

This fast-growing deciduous tree makes a fine specimen for a large garden, reaching 40ft (12m) in 20 years. Its stately form and strength contribute to the tree's beauty. The leaves are distinctively four-lobed and glossy green, turning butter yellow in autumn. The spectacular flowers are greenish-yellow with orange centers, reminiscent of tulips, and give the plant its common name. An alternative is 'Aureomarginatum', a variegated form with golden-edged leaves. It flowers at an earlier age than the species.

z 4-9 sun u.h. 200ft (60m)

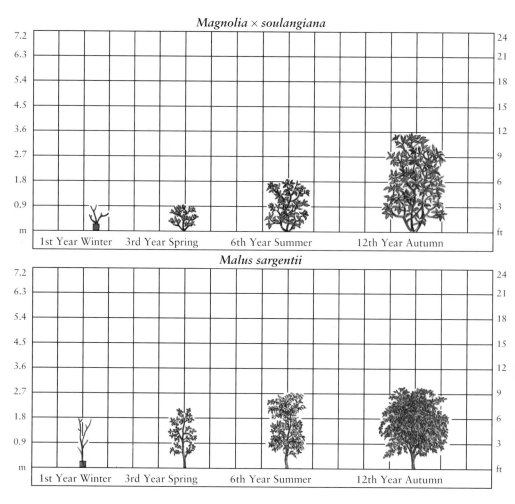

Magnolia × soulangiana

1st Year Winter   3rd Year Spring   6th Year Summer   12th Year Autumn

Malus sargentii

1st Year Winter   3rd Year Spring   6th Year Summer   12th Year Autumn

Magnolia × soulangiana

Saucer magnolia

Enormous flowers characterize this deciduous plant. It makes a small tree up to 16ft (5m) tall in 20 years but is often grown as a large shrub. The erect tulip-shaped, waxy white, scented flowers bloom in early spring; they are nearly 6in (15cm) across. Dark green oval leaves, 3 to 6in (7.5-15cm) long, appear in late spring. There are several pink forms, the best being 'Lennei', with blooms that are rose-purple on the outside and creamy-white inside. The leaves are larger than *soulangiana* but the plant is smaller.

z 5-8 sun or partial shade u.h. 33ft (10m)

Malus sargentii

Sargent crab apple

This deciduous tree, one of the smallest ornamental crab apples, reaches about 10ft (3m) in 15 years. In spring it is a cloud of small white scented flowers; in autumn it bears tiny red fruit. The cultivar 'Rosea' is slightly more vigorous and has pale pink flowers that are rosy in bud. 'Red Jade' is a little larger and often has a slightly lop-sided habit, giving it an Oriental appearance, with blush pink flowers and small red crabs. The cultivar 'Golden Hornet' bears yellow fruit that lasts well into the winter.

z 4-8 sun or partial shade u.h. 10ft (3m)

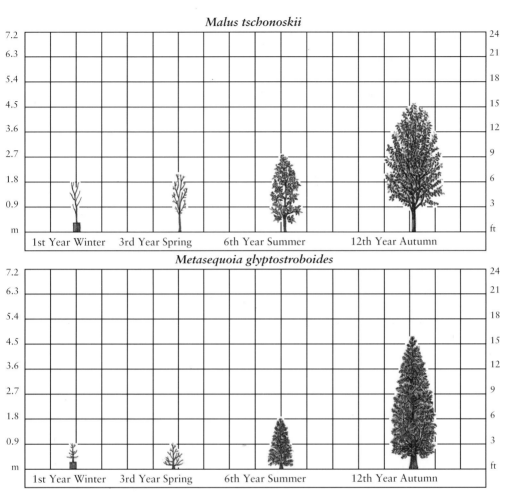

Malus tschonoskii

Tschonoski crab apple
This large deciduous tree reaches 20ft (6m) or more in 20 years and is grown for its autumn color. It is often used as a street tree as in the early years it has a particularly upright pyramidal shape that broadens as the tree matures. The young stems are attractively downy white and the oval or rounded leaves, 2 to 4in (5-10cm) long, are velvety white beneath but turn vibrant shades of orange, red, purple and yellow in the autumn. The small pink-tinged white flowers are occasionally followed by yellow-orange fruit.

z 4-8 sun or partial shade u.h. 40ft (12m)

Metasequoia glyptostroboides

Dawn redwood
Until the mid-20th century, when it was rediscovered growing in China, this deciduous conifer tree was only known as a fossil. As a specimen it makes a narrow, very regular pyramid reaching 36ft (11m) in 25 years, with a canopy of feathery foliage that is bright green in spring and golden yellow in the autumn. The trunk is tapered and covered with cinnamon-brown bark. It grows best in a moist position and withstands pollution well. For boggy conditions *Taxodium distichum*, the swamp cypress, is best.

z 5-8 sun u.h. 100ft (30m)

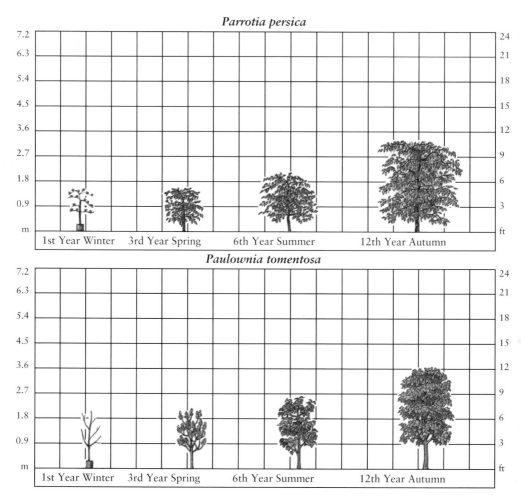

Parrotia persica

Persian parrotia

Stiff branches characterize the habit of this tree. It reaches 16ft (5m) with a spread of about 15ft (4.5m) in 20 years. Discreet red-stamened flowers appear in late winter, set off by the gray flaking bark. In spring, leaves unfurl reddish-purple and turn dark green. However, this deciduous tree is best known for its striking autumn tints of deep yellow, carmine and rusty orange. It is tolerant of alkaline conditions but colors best in moist, well-drained, acid soil.

z 5 sun u.h. 40ft (12m)

Paulownia tomentosa

Princess tree

This gaunt tree reaches 16ft (5m) in 20 years. It has lobed deciduous leaves up to 10in (25cm) long that often come after the flowers. The blue-mauve foxglove-like panicles of flowers appear on mature trees in late spring, after a mild winter: the tree benefits from shelter. It can also be grown as a foliage plant, if the stems are cut back hard in the spring. A useful alternative is **Catalpa bignonioides**, the Indian bean tree, which has spreading branches, heart-shaped leaves, panicles of white flowers and bean-like seed pods.

z 7-9 sun u.h. 50ft (15m)

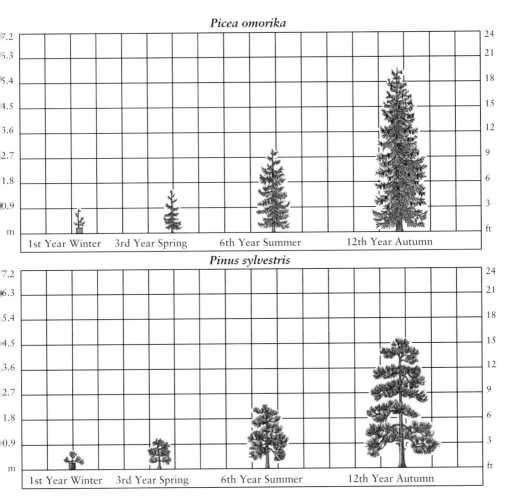

Picea omorika

1st Year Winter	3rd Year Spring	6th Year Summer	12th Year Autumn

Pinus sylvestris

1st Year Winter	3rd Year Spring	6th Year Summer	12th Year Autumn

Picea omorika

Serbian spruce

This is among the most graceful and hardy of the evergreen conifers and reaches about 20ft (6m) in 20 years. It has a slender profile with short branches that curve down and turn up at their tips. The needles are about ½in (1.2cm) long, dark green above with a central white stripe beneath and often a blue tip. The dark bluish cones are about 2in (5cm) long. The Colorado spruce, **P. pungens**, is slower-growing but makes a taller, more conical tree. It has blue, angled needles and purplish-brown cones, 4in (10cm) long.

z 4-8 sun or partial shade u.h. 90ft (27m)

Pinus sylvestris

Scotch pine

Quantities of this tree have been planted as windbreaks and are recognizable by their distinctive tall, gaunt, bare, reddy-brown trunks below a flat canopy of black-green needles. The trees grow quickly, reaching 30ft (9m) or more in 20 years. They are conical when young, losing their lower branches as they age. The dark grayish-green needles grow in pairs, 2 to 3in (5-7.5cm) long or more, and are often twisted. The brown cones are 1 to 3in (2.5-7.5cm) long. Pines grow tallest in well-drained, humus-rich soil.

z 3-8 sun u.h. 100ft (30m)

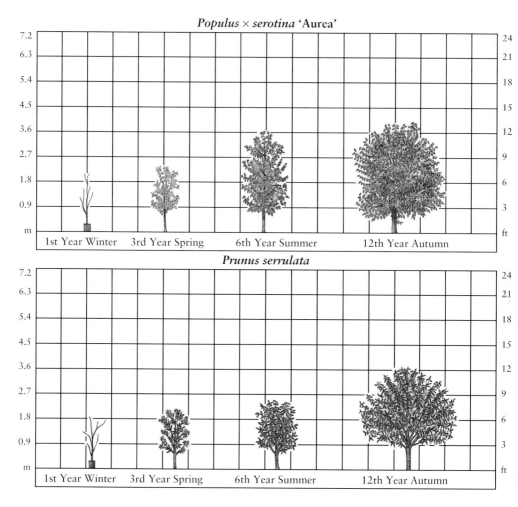

Populus × serotina 'Aurea'

| | 1st Year Winter | 3rd Year Spring | 6th Year Summer | 12th Year Autumn |

Prunus serrulata

| | 1st Year Winter | 3rd Year Spring | 6th Year Summer | 12th Year Autumn |

Populus × serotina 'Aurea'

Carolina poplar

This tree is sometimes classified as *P. × canadensis* 'Serotina Aurea'. It is vigorous and grows to 30ft (9m) in 20 years. Poplars like plenty of moisture and their roots can cause damage to foundations and drains. The young pyramidal tree develops a densely branched rounded canopy as it matures. The broadly oval and pointed leaves are clear yellow in spring, green-up through the summer and turn a rich yellow again in the autumn. The more upright *P. balsamifera* will reach 40ft (12m) in 20 years.

z 4-8 sun u.h. 150ft (45m)

Prunus serrulata

A small flowering cherry, which reaches 25ft (7.5m) in 20 years, with arching branches and shiny mahogany bark that peels horizontally. The species has pointed oval leaves and small white or pink-tinted blossoms in spring. Hybrids such as **'Kanzan'**, the most famous double pink, **'Tai Haku'**, the great white cherry (with single flowers), and **'Shiro-fugen'**, perhaps the best with bluey-pink flowers in bud that open white and age back to pink, are spectacular Japanese garden cherries. They often have coppery young growth and bright autumn color.

z 5-8 sun or partial shade u.h. 33ft (10m)

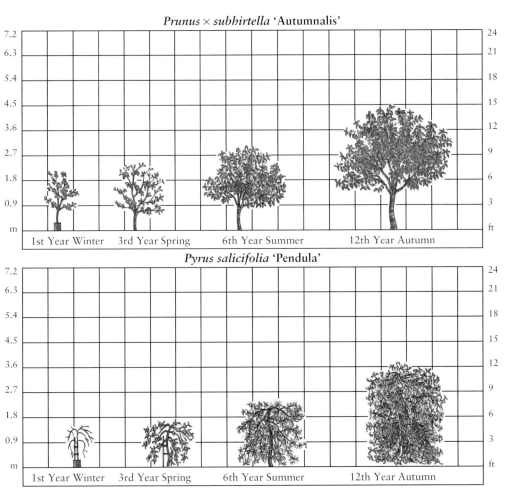

Prunus × subhirtella 'Autumnalis'

| 1st Year Winter | 3rd Year Spring | 6th Year Summer | 12th Year Autumn |

Pyrus salicifolia 'Pendula'

| 1st Year Winter | 3rd Year Spring | 6th Year Summer | 12th Year Autumn |

Prunus × *subhirtella* 'Autumnalis'

Winter-flowering cherry

Most commonly grown as a single-stem small tree up to 20ft (6m) in 20 years, this plant can occasionally be found as a multi-stemmed shrub. The small white flowers (pink in bud) open in late autumn, at first thinly, but in increasing quantities, and last through the winter, dwindling as spring approaches. They will be damaged in very cold weather but the tree will bloom with increased vigor once the cold spell passes. The light deciduous canopy of mid-green foliage turns orange and bronze in autumn.

z 5-8 sun or partial shade u.h. 25ft (7.5m)

Pyrus salicifolia 'Pendula'

Weeping willow-leaved pear

This small tree, which reaches 15ft (4.5m) in 15 years, has pendulous branches that sweep to the ground and is best planted as a specimen in a lawn or courtyard. The narrow, willow-like deciduous leaves are covered with gray down in spring and turn a soft green in summer. Creamy-white flowers are followed by small pear-shaped fruit. **P. *calleryana***, the wild Chinese pear, is tall and narrow and also suitable for a restricted space. It has white flowers and, in autumn, purplish-red leaves and small round light orange fruit.

z 5-8 sun u.h. 15ft (4.5m)

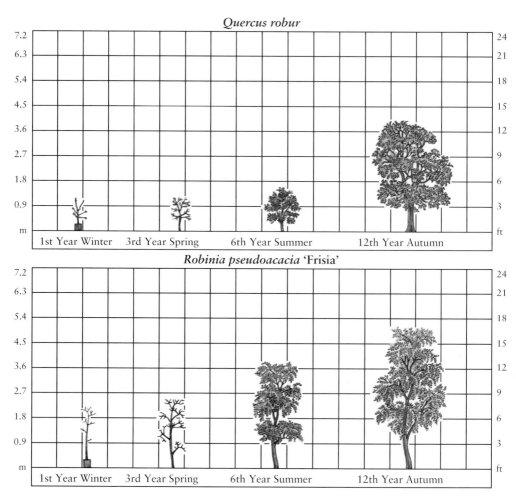

Quercus robur

1st Year Winter	3rd Year Spring	6th Year Summer	12th Year Autumn

Robinia pseudoacacia 'Frisia'

1st Year Winter	3rd Year Spring	6th Year Summer	12th Year Autumn

Quercus robur

English oak

This tree only puts on significant growth after eight years or so, but it will reach 33 to 40ft (10-12m) in 20 years. Both **Q. cerris**, Turkey oak, and **Q. rubra**, red oak, are quicker to establish and faster-growing, reaching 45ft (14m) in 20 years. The evergreen **Q. ilex**, holm oak, only reaches 20ft (6m) in the same time. All develop into very tall trees, suitable only for large gardens. Q. robur has a wide crown with lobed pale green leaves that turn russet in the autumn, lasting into the winter. Older trees produce acorns.

z 5-8 sun or partial shade u.h. 100ft (30m)

Robinia pseudoacacia 'Frisia'

Golden false acacia

A slender angular tree of modest height, ideal for a small garden. It grows quickly when young and reaches 20ft (6m) in 20 years. The pinnate leaves open late, a pale yellow, turning green in summer and rich butter yellow in autumn. They have orangey petioles. The tree has red thorns and white pea-like flowers which are not as plentiful as in the species. The golden honey-locust, **Gleditsia triacanthos 'Sunburst'**, is slower to establish but reaches similar heights; it is thornless and has a much rounder habit.

z 6-9 sun u.h. 50ft (15m)

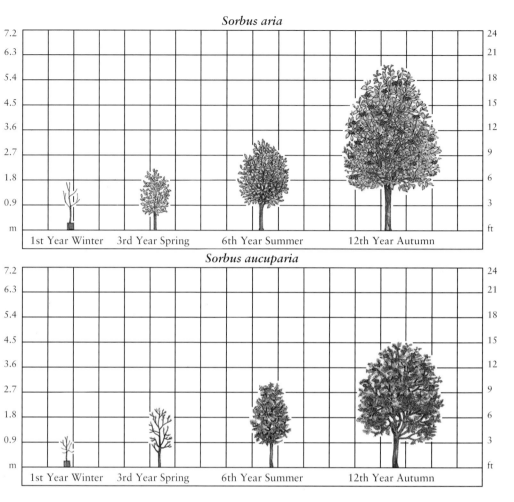

Sorbus aria

Whitebeam

This tree has an upright habit with a rounded crown of large leaves, up to 5in (12.5cm) long, that are bright green above and downy gray beneath. The early summer panicles of white flowers are about 4in (10cm) wide and are followed by conspicuous bunches of scarlet fruit. *S.* × *hostii* is much smaller, to 13ft (4m), with pink flowers and orange berries. In areas where pests that bore into wood are a problem, the Korean mountain ash (*S. alnifolia*) is to be recommended. These plants are tolerant of dry soils.

z 6-9 sun or partial shade u.h. 65ft (19.5m)

Sorbus aucuparia

Mountain ash or rowan

This tree has pinnate leaves composed of toothed leaflets with orangey tints in the autumn. It grows to 23ft (7m) in 20 years, with an upright habit and narrowly oval or rounded head. The spring panicles of white blossom turn to great bunches of berries in shades of red and orange in mid- to late summer. The hybrid '**Joseph Rock**' has pale pink flowers, yellow to rust berries and purple and copper autumn tints. In *S. cashmiriana* the fruit is white and, less attractive to birds, stays on the tree until the winter.

z 2-8 sun or partial shade u.h. 50ft (15m)

Left: The modern hybrid shrub rose 'Marguerite Hilling' is a sport of 'Nevada' that quickly reaches 6ft (1.8m) or more. Dark pink buds open to fragrant semi-double pink recurrent flowers.

Right: The evergreen *Photinia × fraseri* 'Birmingham' is a recently introduced hybrid that has brilliant red young growth, similar to that of *Pieris*. Unlike *Pieris* it does not require acid soil and it is a larger plant, reaching 7ft (2.1m) by 5ft (1.5m) in ten years.

Shrubs

Shrubs have many attributes which qualify them to form the backbone planting of a garden. Generally speaking, they are undemanding to grow and are reasonably long-lived; some are outstandingly beautiful either all year round or at a particular season. Shrubs are available in many different sizes. Most are sufficiently large to give substance to a garden; these can be used to form a dense backdrop to smaller, slower-growing varieties.

Some shrubs reach the size of small trees, others can be tiny. Even within the same genera there are extremes. For example, *Cotoneaster* 'Cornubia' will reach 10ft (3m) in twelve years, while the dwarf *C. dammeri* is never taller than 4in (10cm). However, most species will reach some 8ft (2.4m) at maturity, provided that the soil and climate are appropriate. There is a shrub for almost every garden soil. In sharply drained alkaline soils brooms, rock-roses, daphnes and lavender will feel most at home; on the other hand rhododendrons, pieris, kalmia and camellias are happiest in organically rich, acid, moisture-retentive soils.

The ornamental qualities of shrubs are equally varied: attractive habits, foliage, blossom, fruit and bark can all be enhanced by careful association. For example, the dense purple foliage of *Cotinus coggygria* 'Notcutt's Variety' is set off by the silver-variegated *Cornus alba* 'Elegantissima' and complemented in the early summer by the deep purple double blooms of scented lilac *Syringa vulgaris* 'Katherine Havemeyer'.

Shrubs are very versatile garden plants. They can be grouped in shrubberies, used as isolated specimens or employed in mixed borders with herbaceous perennials, ground cover, bulbs and annuals. Some can be successfully coupled with a climber, the one enhancing the other. Summer-flowering clematis work well with shrubs. For example, *Clematis* 'Lasurstern' looks stunning with the white ball-shaped blossoms of *Viburnum opulus* 'Sterile'; the mauvey-pink and white flowers of *C. viticella* 'Minuet' associate perfectly with the purple foliage of *Cotinus coggygria* 'Royal Purple'. A clematis adds to the interest of a shrub that has only one season of glory: *C.* 'Perle d'Azur' is happy climbing through the dark green foliage of *Corylus avellana* 'Contorta'

in the summer; the white 'Marie Boisselot' ornaments the plain summer foliage of winter-flowering honeysuckle, *Lonicera fragrantissima*; the early-flowering *C. macropetala* threads its nodding blossoms successfully through the autumn-flowering *Clerodendron trichotomum*. Other climbers that can be grown through shrubs include sweet peas and the flame nasturtium, *Tropaeolum speciosum*.

Although shrubs are easy to grow, they need regular pruning to maintain a good shape and to get the best possible display year after year. When the plant

The evergreen *Pyracantha* 'Mohave' and the deciduous purple-leaved *Berberis atrocarpa* are both vigorous shrubs that display berries well into the winter. They are suitable for a large garden as tall, background planting in a shrubbery. In the foreground is the evergreen *Viburnum tinus* 'Gwenllian' which has pale pink flowers in late winter, followed by a plentiful crop of black berries. All these shrubs do well in shady conditions and so are very useful for planting under the canopy of tall trees.

is well established in the garden (after four or five years), pruning can take place just once a year. Generally speaking, shrubs that flower in summer do so on the current year's wood and should be pruned at the end of the summer or, where the winters are hard, at the beginning of spring when any frost-damaged wood can be cut out. Spring-flowering shrubs bear blooms on the previous year's wood and should be pruned immediately after the flowers have faded, so that the plant has the longest possible time to grow sufficient wood for the following season's blossoms.

However, if all the flower stems are cut off, there will be no fruit in the autumn. If the fruits are decorative, a good compromise is to prune out only half or a third of the flowering stems. Shrubs grown for the effect of their winter bark, such as *Cornus alba* 'Sibirica', *C. stolonifera* and *Salis alba* 'Britzensis', should be pruned back in the spring.

It is important to look out for weak and diseased or dead branches throughout a shrub's life. These are often easiest to identify in the late summer when the plant is still in leaf but growth is slowing down. Any unwanted branches

should be cut out and burned to prevent the spread of disease. Awkwardly placed branches should be cut right down to the main stem to keep the shape of the shrub balanced. Again, it is a good idea to do this in summer as any drastic winter pruning encourages vigorous growth the following season. If you want strong growth (if, for example, you inherit an overgrown plant that needs to generate new growth), then by all means prune in winter.

It is advisable when pruning to bear in mind the effect you want to achieve once the plant has grown back. Going over a shrub with shears to keep it within bounds will result in a plant that looks like a half-hearted topiary specimen. It is best to cut the most vigorous shoots right down to ground level, leaving only a few well-placed stems that are not overstepping the mark. The plant will soon fill out into a healthy, balanced shape.

A shrubbery will take recognizable shape within five to seven years of planting and after about ten to twelve years it will reach its prime. By this time each plant should be just about touching the neighboring shrubs but should retain its own shape. For another five years or so the shrubbery will continue to look mature and at its best, but after that it will begin to look overgrown and start to degenerate as some shrubs become dominant and swamp others. At this point, either the

Left: The vibrant foliage of the purple smoke bush, *Cotinus coggygria* 'Royal Purple', is complemented by frothy purple blossom in summer. This plant grows to 6ft (1.8m) in ten years but can be contained by hard pruning in early spring.
Above: *Elaeagnus pungens* 'Maculata' is a slow-growing shrub with large yellow stains on the elongated leaves. This striking foliage brightens up a dull day or a partially shaded corner.

Kerria japonica 'Flore Pleno' is covered with brilliant yellow double flowers in spring. This vigorous bush has tall, erect green stems that reach 6 to 8ft (1.8-2.4m) in tens years and spread by suckers. It is a good shrub for a shady wall. The single form, *K. japonica*, has an arching habit and is less vigorous.

smaller specimens should be removed if height is most desirable, or the more dominant shrubs should go, allowing the shrouded shrubs to fulfil their potential. To avoid a great upheaval in the garden, replanting should be done in stages. Therefore, it is important to identify plants that may need replacing in a year's time, or more.

The lifespan of a shrubbery or group of shrubs will depend on the rate of growth of individual plants and the density of planting. Ideally, the probable spread of shrubs at twelve years should be used as a guide for the distance between shrubs at planting time, but in order to achieve a substantial effect more quickly it is usually worth planting them slightly more closely. This will mean that the most vigorous specimens will require fairly hard pruning to keep them within bounds. When growth is just beginning the spaces between the shrubs should be furnished with ground-covering plants, bulbs and some annuals to prevent weeds from competing with the young shrubs. These fillers must be removed when they are no longer required.

When the shrubs are well established, an application of small quantities of a pre-emergent herbicide will prevent weeds from germinating; most (but not all shrubs) will be unaffected by this. Alternatively, if herbicides are not favored, a generous mulch of pulverized fresh bark or of gravel will inhibit most weeds.

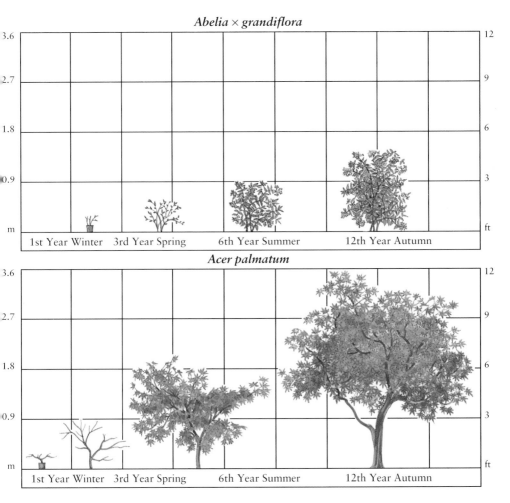

Abelia × grandiflora

1st Year Winter	3rd Year Spring	6th Year Summer	12th Year Autumn

Acer palmatum

1st Year Winter	3rd Year Spring	6th Year Summer	12th Year Autumn

Abelia × grandiflora

This is a useful shrub that flowers from late summer into the autumn when little else makes a show. It has graceful, slender, arching branches that reach 4ft (1.2m) or so high and as much across, in ten years. It is deciduous in all but the mildest areas and does best in a sheltered site. The pale pink, slightly scented flowers stand out against the bright green foliage for several weeks. There is a yellow variegated form, 'Variegata'.

z 6 sun u.h. 5-6½ft (1.5-2m) ▲

Acer palmatum

Japanese maple

In its native habitat this plant will grow into a tree, but in cultivation it is so slow-growing that it is best treated as a shrub. The species has large palmate leaves with five or seven lobes 2 to 4in (5-10cm) wide that turn scarlet in the autumn. The tiny summer flowers are purplish and are followed by keys. **'Atropurpureum'** reaches 6ft (1.8m) and has rich red-purple foliage; **'Dissectum'** is very slow-growing, up to 2ft by 4ft (60 × 120cm), with finely cut bright green foliage that turns browny-yellow. Acid soil is best.

z 5-9 partial shade u.h. 40ft (12m) ▲

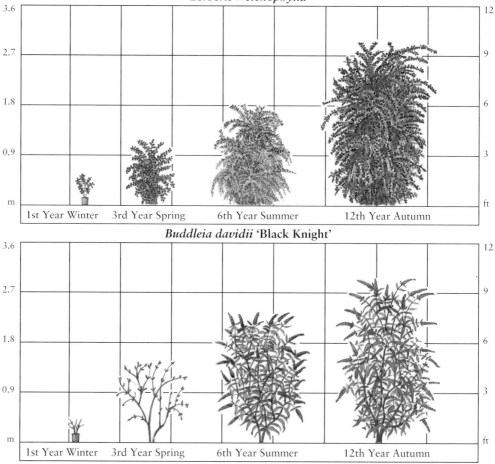

Berberis × *stenophylla*

3.6					12
2.7					9
1.8					6
0.9					3
m	1st Year Winter	3rd Year Spring	6th Year Summer	12th Year Autumn	ft

Buddleia davidii 'Black Knight'

3.6					12
2.7					9
1.8					6
0.9					3
m	1st Year Winter	3rd Year Spring	6th Year Summer	12th Year Autumn	ft

Berberis × *stenophylla*

The arching branches of this evergreen barberry are laden in late spring with tiny, orangey-yellow, scented, bell-shaped flowers. These are followed by blue-black fruit in the autumn. It grows quickly, reaching 10ft by 6½ft (3 × 2m), making a dense thicket or informal hedge. The narrow, 1in (2.5cm), dark green spiny leaves make it impenetrable. In colder areas the deciduous *B.* × *ottawensis* 'Atropurpurea' makes a suitable alternative, achieving the same height, with dark purple foliage and pale yellow flowers. (▲)

z 5-8 sun or partial shade u.h. 10ft (3m) ●

Buddleia davidii 'Black Knight'

Buddleias will grow in the poorest soil and they can be something of a weed. The most common species, *B. davidii*, has dull green oval leaves and flowers ranging from rich dark velvety purple ('Black Knight') to violet blue (**'Empire Blue'**) and white (**'White Profusion'** or 'Peace'). They make a beautiful show for nearly a month in the summer and attract butterflies, hence their common name, butterfly bush. *B. alternifolia* has pale mauve fragrant flowers in early summer but can make a tangled mess unless pruned and trained.

z 5-9 sun or partial shade u.h. 10-16ft (3-5m) ■

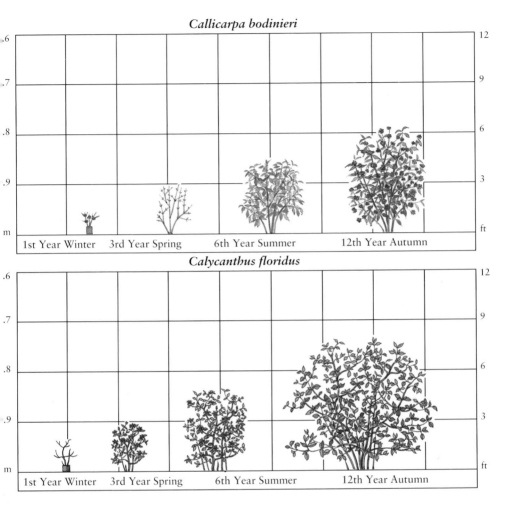

Callicarpa bodinieri

1st Year Winter 3rd Year Spring 6th Year Summer 12th Year Autumn

Calycanthus floridus

1st Year Winter 3rd Year Spring 6th Year Summer 12th Year Autumn

Callicarpa bodinieri

This vigorous shrub has a bushy upright habit, with stiff stems a little over 6ft (1.8m) tall and a spread of 4ft (1.2m) in ten years. The dull green lanceolate leaves are between 2 and 5in (5-12.5cm) long, and acquire a hint of purple in autumn. Clusters of small mauve flowers appear in summer and are followed by the much prized purple berries which may last several months after the leaves have dropped. The cultivar **'Profusion'** is particularly floriferous. These plants prefer acid soils, and poor soils should be improved with a little peat or leaf mold.

z 6-8 sun or partial shade u.h. 6½ft (2m) ▲

Calycanthus floridus

Carolina allspice
A beautifully disciplined shrub which makes a neat rounded bush up to 7ft (2.1m) tall and 8ft (2.4m) wide in ten years. It has glossy apple green oval leaves 2 to 6in (5-15cm) long which set off the small burgundy-colored flowers that have many ribbon-shaped petals and an unforgettable spicy fragrance. The California allspice, **C. occidentalis**, is similar in every part but somewhat less hardy. Grow both forms in moisture-retentive soil.

z 4-9 sun u.h. 10ft (3m) ▲

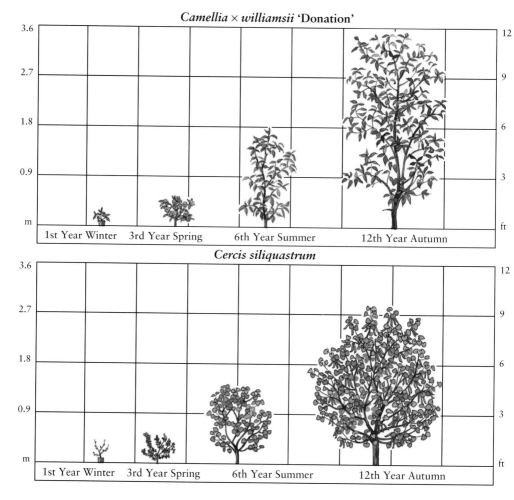

Camellia × williamsii 'Donation'

1st Year Winter   3rd Year Spring   6th Year Summer   12th Year Autumn

Cercis siliquastrum

1st Year Winter   3rd Year Spring   6th Year Summer   12th Year Autumn

Camellia × williamsii

Camellias need shelter or a mild climate, and acid soil. In winter or early spring their evergreen dark glossy foliage highlights velvety petaled flowers in red, pink and white tones. Williamsii hybrids (between the species C. *japonica* and C. *saluenensis*) are among the best and hardiest, reaching 10ft (3m) in ten years. Flowers range from white (**'Francis Hanger'**) to pale pink (**'J.C. Williams'**) to darker pink (**'Donation'**). Hybrids of **C. *sasanqua*** and **C. *japonica*** are not all fully hardy. In cold areas grow camellias in tubs that can be kept frost-free.

z 7-9 partial shade u.h. 20ft (6m) ▲

Cercis siliquastrum

Judas tree
A small tree in the warmth of its natural Mediterranean habitat, in cultivation this is most commonly found as a large multi-stemmed shrub, reaching 8ft by 7ft (2.4 × 2.1m) in ten years. Clusters of bright red-purple pea-like flowers appear in late spring on the branches and even on the trunk. The heart-shaped glaucous leaves follow in early summer. The Chinese redbud, **C. *chinensis***, and the eastern redbud, **C. *canadensis***, are hardier, from z 6 and z 4 respectively. Grow in well-drained soil, protected from cold winds.

z 7-9 sun u.h. 40ft (12m) ▲

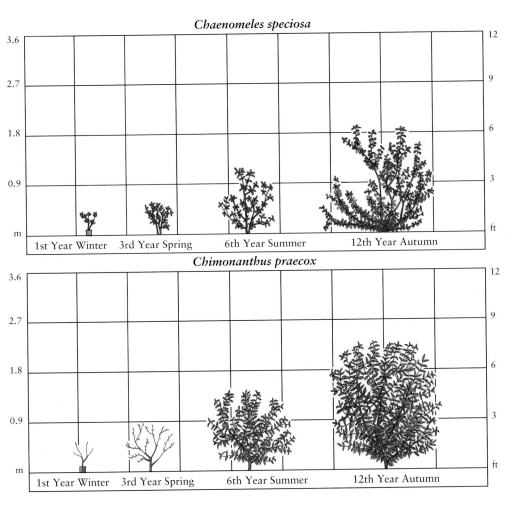

Chaenomeles speciosa

1st Year Winter   3rd Year Spring   6th Year Summer   12th Year Autumn

Chimonanthus praecox

1st Year Winter   3rd Year Spring   6th Year Summer   12th Year Autumn

Chaenomeles speciosa

The ornamental quince, often known as japonica, grows well against a wall, reaching 6ft (1.8m) in ten years. The rich vermilion flowers open in early spring and are often followed by plump, yellow fruits in the autumn. Cultivars include the white '**Jet Trail**', up to 8ft (2.4m), the pale pink and white '**Moerloesii**', with an arching habit to 4ft by 5ft (1.2 × 1.5m), and the semi-double crimson '**Simonii**', low-growing up to 3ft (90cm). Prune selectively in spring after flowering to ensure upward growth, otherwise stems tend to grow forward from the base.

z 4-8 partial shade u.h. 7ft (2.1m) ●

Chimonanthus praecox

Wintersweet

This fine shrub does well on a warm wall and flowers in the coldest months of the winter. It is deciduous, growing to 7ft (2.1m) in ten years, with deep green, narrow leaves that provide a good background for clematis to grow through during the spring and summer. The delicate, fragrant, palest cream flowers have a maroon to purple center and bloom on the bare twigs. '**Grandiflorus**' has deeper yellow flowers and a larger stain and '**Luteus**' has later-opening, waxy yellow unstained flowers.

z 6-9 sun u.h. 8ft (2.4m) ▲

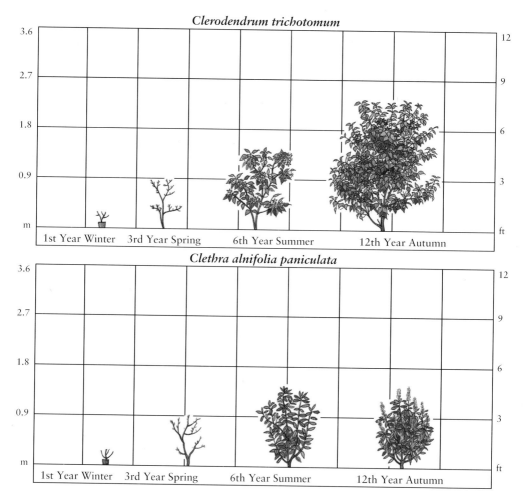

Clerodendrum trichotomum

1st Year Winter   3rd Year Spring   6th Year Summer   12th Year Autumn

Clethra alnifolia paniculata

1st Year Winter   3rd Year Spring   6th Year Summer   12th Year Autumn

Clerodendrum trichotomum

This deciduous shrub makes a rounded, suckering specimen nearly 8ft by 6ft (2.4 × 1.8m) in ten years. Random pithy branches bear 6in (15cm) oval leaves. These are dark green, with a hint of purple in autumn, and have a strong smell. Blossoms appear in late summer: little white stars are set off by maroon calyxes. The plant's chief glory is its fruits that follow immediately after the flowers. The electric blue berries stand out against the remaining calyxes, now bright red. The sub-species, *fargesii*, is hardier and more fruitful. Both need good drainage.

z 6-9 sun u.h. 20ft (6m) ▲

Clethra alnifolia paniculata

Sweet pepperbush

A native of swampy ground and damp woodlands, this is a useful late summer flowering shrub for light, moist, acid soils. It makes a suckering, dense thicket, reaching some 5ft by 3ft (1.5m × 90cm) in ten years. The attractive deciduous foliage is bright green in spring and summer, yellow and orange in autumn. Upright panicles of white flowers fill the late summer and autumn air with a strong fragrance; these are followed in warm climates by black fruits that resemble peppercorns. Pink forms are available.

z 3-9 partial shade u.h. 6-10ft (1.8-3m) ▲

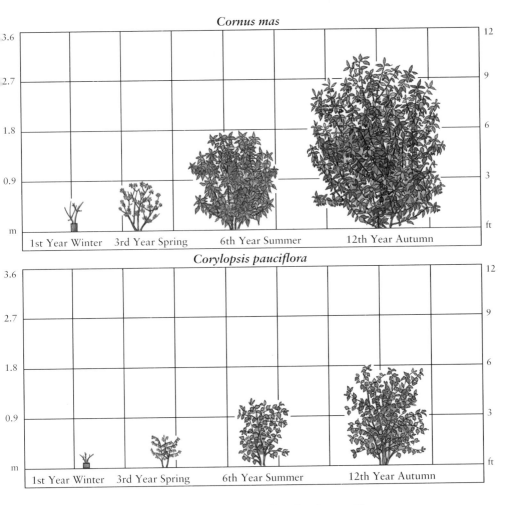

Cornus mas

| 1st Year Winter | 3rd Year Spring | 6th Year Summer | 12th Year Autumn |

Corylopsis pauciflora

| 1st Year Winter | 3rd Year Spring | 6th Year Summer | 12th Year Autumn |

Cornus mas

Cornelian cherry

This is one of my favorite shrubs. It has an open twiggy habit making a wide spreading plant 10ft by 6ft (3 × 1.8m) in ten years. The small, pale yellow, early spring blossom studs the bare branches. The oval leaves, 2 to 4in (5-10cm) long, are dark green and turn orangey-red in the autumn. In a warm climate, small cherry-like edible fruits appear in autumn. This dogwood is also suitable as a hedge which should be pruned in early summer.

z 4-8 sun or partial shade u.h. 23ft (7m) ▲

Corylopsis pauciflora

Winterhazel

A graceful arching habit characterizes this low-growing shrub. It will reach 6ft (1.8m) in height, 5ft (1.5m) in spread, in ten years. The pale yellow, scented, bell-shaped flowers open in racemes in early spring before the young pink foliage. The rather dull leaves, which resemble those of hazel, can be enlivened in the summer by growing a large-flowering clematis through them. Grow in humus-rich soil.

z 5-9 partial shade u.h. 6½ft (2m) ▲

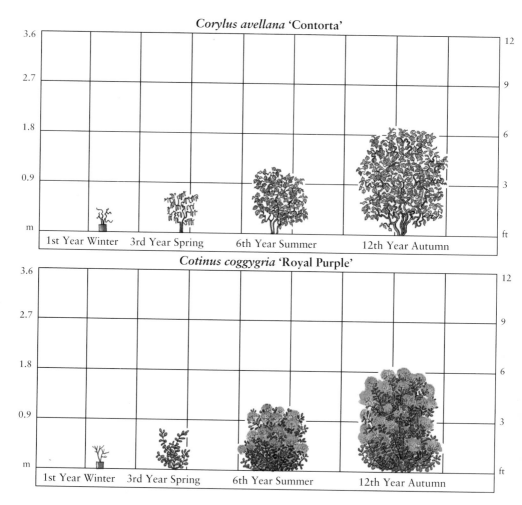

Corylus avellana 'Contorta'

1st Year Winter   3rd Year Spring   6th Year Summer   12th Year Autumn

Cotinus coggygria 'Royal Purple'

1st Year Winter   3rd Year Spring   6th Year Summer   12th Year Autumn

Corylus avellana 'Contorta'
Harry Lauder's walking stick
This hazel makes a dense bush up to 7ft by 5ft (2.1 × 1.5m) in ten years. It has extraordinary twisted branches that stand out against snow and make a feature of the plant in the winter. In early spring yellow catkins cover the plant and are followed by a heavy canopy of dark green leaves, similar in shape to those of the ordinary hazel but crinkly. There is a form of Peking willow that also has corkscrew-like stems: *Salix matsudana* **'Tortuosa'** makes a tree 33 to 40ft (10-12m) tall.

z 3-8 sun or shade u.h. 10ft (3m) ▲

Cotinus coggygria 'Royal Purple'
Smoke bush
This striking purple plant forms a neat mound 6ft by 5ft (1.8 × 1.5m) in ten years. The alternating rounded leaves are about 2½in (6.5cm) long and open bright warm red-purple, deepening through the season to a dark velvety maroon. Feathery panicles of pink blossom create an aura around the plant in mid- to late summer. This plant is a perfect foil for silver variegated plants and purple flowering shrubs. It should be grown in well-drained soil.

z 4-8 sun u.h. 10ft (3m) ◆

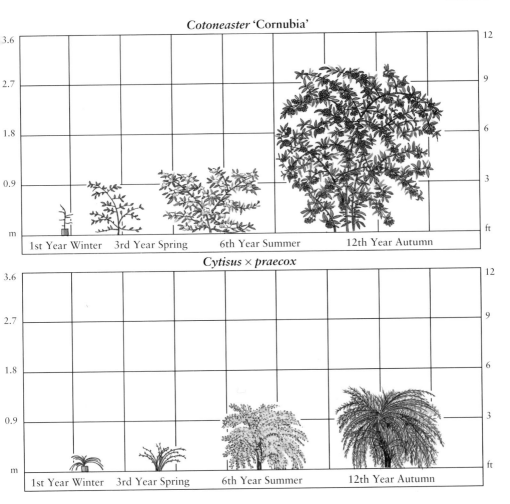

Cotoneaster 'Cornubia'

3.6 — 2.7 — 1.8 — 0.9 — m
12 — 9 — 6 — 3 — ft

1st Year Winter 3rd Year Spring 6th Year Summer 12th Year Autumn

Cytisus × *praecox*

3.6 — 2.7 — 1.8 — 0.9 — m
12 — 9 — 6 — 3 — ft

1st Year Winter 3rd Year Spring 6th Year Summer 12th Year Autumn

Cotoneaster 'Cornubia'

There are many species of cotoneaster, some evergreen, most deciduous. They make large, mostly graceful shrubs, such as **C. franchettii**, or smaller ground-hugging ones such as **C. horizontalis** or **C. dammeri**. Most have white flowers in early summer, followed by a copious crop of orange to red berries. The semi-evergreen hybrid 'Cornubia' reaches 10ft by 10ft (3 × 3m) in ten years. It has 4in (10cm) long deep green leaves and large bunches of red autumn berries.
C. 'Rothschildianus' has yellow fruit;
C. divaricatus has scarlet autumn foliage.

z 7-9 sun or shade u.h. 20ft (6m) ▲

Cytisus × *praecox*

Warminster broom

This makes a rounded bush with green angular stems that resemble a tousled mop of hair. It reaches 4ft by 5ft (1.2 × 1.5m) in eight years. It is spectacular for at least three weeks in late spring when pale yellow blooms cover the cascading twiggy branches; the scent is not very pleasant. The new shoots are silky green and the small deciduous leaves drop early in the season. Cultivars include the original hybrid **'Warminster'**, **'Allgold'**, deeper in color, and the paler **'Moonlight'**. Grow in well-drained soil.

z 6-8 sun u.h. 5-6ft (1.5-1.8m) ●

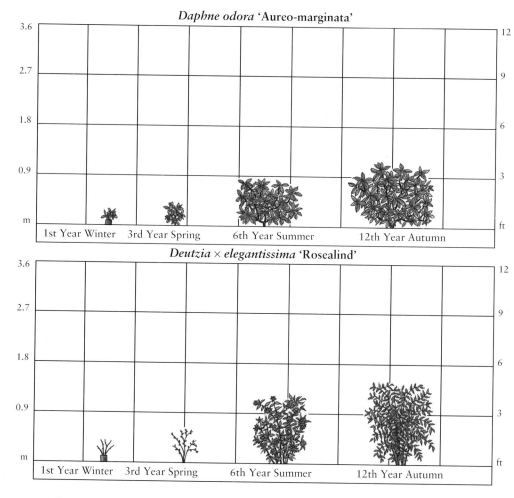

Daphne odora 'Aureo-marginata'

1st Year Winter   3rd Year Spring   6th Year Summer   12th Year Autumn

Deutzia × *elegantissima* 'Rosealind'

1st Year Winter   3rd Year Spring   6th Year Summer   12th Year Autumn

Daphne odora 'Aureo-marginata'

All daphnes are scented in early spring but this is perhaps the most aromatic. It has a rounded habit, reaching 4ft by 5ft (1.2 × 1.5m) in ten years. The evergreen leaves have pale yellow variegations and the flowers open pink and fade to white. The deciduous mezereon, **D. mezereum**, is exceptionally hardy (to −30°C/−22°F) but slower growing. It has gray-green foliage, purple-red spring blossom and highly poisonous red berries. **D.** × **burkwoodii** 'Carol Mackie' has gold-edged leaves and is even hardier. All daphnes like well-drained soil that does not dry out.

z 8-10 sun u.h. 4-5ft (1.2-1.5m) ▲

Deutzia × *elegantissima* 'Rosealind'

This easily grown, reliable shrub flowers profusely in summer. The arching stems spread gracefully from the base, reaching 4ft (1.2m) in height. In spring these are covered with dense corymbs of carmine-pink star-shaped flowers. The mid-green slender deciduous leaves are 2 to 3in (5-7.5cm) long. A large-flowered clematis looks attractive growing through the branches, flowering in sequence or to coincide with the shrub. Deutzias do best when sheltered from late spring frosts and should be pruned after flowering by cutting a few stems down to the base.

z 5-8 sun or partial shade u.h. 6ft (1.8m) ●

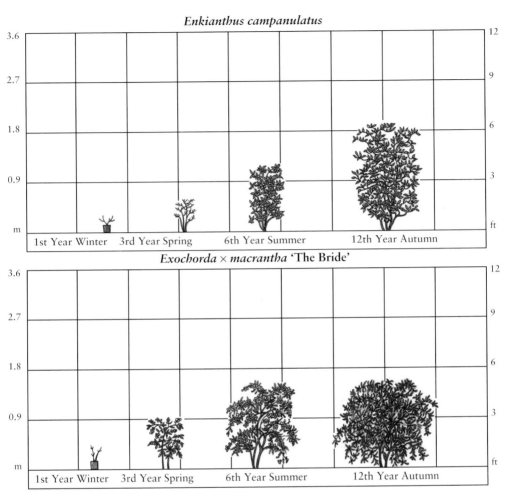

Enkianthus campanulatus

Exochorda × *macrantha* 'The Bride'

1st Year Winter 3rd Year Spring 6th Year Summer 12th Year Autumn

Enkianthus campanulatus

A member of the Ericaceae (heather) family, this shrub requires moisture-retentive acid soil to thrive. It has an upright bushy habit up to 6½ft (2m) high and 4ft (1.2m) wide. In late spring waxy bell-like flowers hang in racemes; the blooms are creamy-yellow with red stripes. The plant's true period of glory comes in autumn when the deciduous glossy green serrated leaves turn vibrant shades of yellow and scarlet. The cultivar 'Red Bells' has more prominent stripes on the flowers.

z 4-8 partial shade or sun u.h. 13-16ft (4-5m) ▲

Exochorda × macrantha 'The Bride'

Pearlbush

This hybrid makes a low, rounded shrub of a rather open, spreading habit, 5ft (1.5m) tall and rather more across. In spring, pearl-like buds open into a mass of white flowers. These are borne in dense, pendulous racemes that last for several weeks, the end blooms opening first. There can be up to ten flowers in each raceme. The deciduous fresh green narrow obovate leaves are 2 to 3in (5-7.5cm) long. This is a perfect shrub through which to grow a large-flowered clematis hybrid for summer interest.

z 5-9 sun or partial shade u.h. 5ft (1.5m) ▲

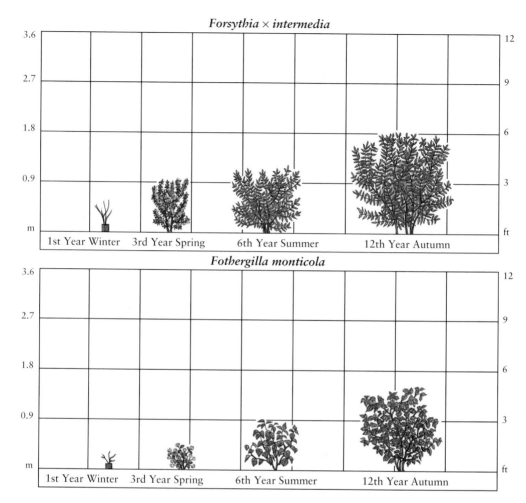

Forsythia × intermedia

1st Year Winter   3rd Year Spring   6th Year Summer   12th Year Autumn

Fothergilla monticola

1st Year Winter   3rd Year Spring   6th Year Summer   12th Year Autumn

Forsythia × intermedia

The bright yellow flowers of forsythia bring a splash of sunshine to early spring. This particularly floriferous deciduous hybrid has rich yellow bell-shaped flowers and grows to about 6ft (1.8m) in ten years. Cultivars include 'Lynwood', 'Spring Glory', 'Spectabilis' and 'Beatrix Farrand', the latter being the most vigorous. *F. suspensa* has long, hanging branches which tend to tangle unless carefully trained. It grows to 12ft by 10ft (3.6 × 3m) in ten years.

z 5-9 sun or partial shade u.h. 8-13ft
(2.4-4m) ●

Fothergilla monticola

Fothergilla has two seasons of interest. The first is spring when it is covered in sweetly scented 1in (2.5cm) creamy-white bottlebrush flower spikes. The deciduous leaves, similar in shape to hazel, are 2 to 4in (5-10cm) long, dark green with a leathery texture in spring, turning warm tones of orange and yellow in the autumn – its second striking phase. *F. monticola* makes a rounded shrub up to 5ft by 5ft (1.5 × 1.5m) in ten years or less. It requires well-drained acid soil to succeed.

z 5-8 sun or partial shade u.h. 5-8ft
(1.5-2.4m) ▲

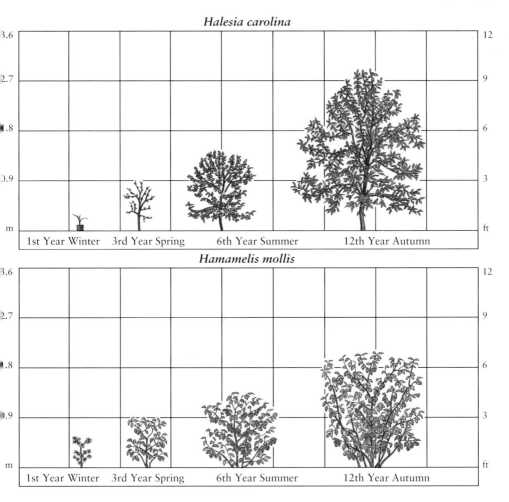

Halesia carolina

3.6					12
2.7					9
1.8					6
0.9					3
m					ft

1st Year Winter   3rd Year Spring   6th Year Summer   12th Year Autumn

Hamamelis mollis

3.6					12
2.7					9
1.8					6
0.9					3
m					ft

1st Year Winter   3rd Year Spring   6th Year Summer   12th Year Autumn

Halesia carolina

Carolina silverbell

A small tree in the wild, this usually makes a large spreading shrub in cultivation, quickly growing to 12ft (3.6m) in ten years. Ideally it should have moist, acid soil with a high organic content, and protection from strong, desiccating winds. The bushy foliage comprises very pale green deciduous leaves, 2 to 5in (5-12.5cm) long, which stand out well against dark evergreens. Pure white bell flowers hang in bunches in early summer, followed by woody, four-cornered fruit, nearly 2in (5cm) long.

z 4-8 sun or partial shade u.h. 30ft (9m) ▲

Hamamelis mollis

Chinese witch hazel

A hardy deciduous ornamental that blooms in late winter. The fragrant flowers, with narrow ribbon-like pale yellow petals, last for nearly a month. The large, rounded, soft-haired leaves turn butter yellow in the autumn. This open, slightly angular shrub reaches 6½ft (2m) and spreads 6ft (1.8m) in ten years. It requires acid to neutral conditions. Together with *H. japonica* it has given rise to the hybrid *H. × intermedia*, with cultivars including '**Diana**', which has orangey-red flowers and autumn foliage.

z 5-8 partial shade or sun u.h. 8ft (2.4m) ▲

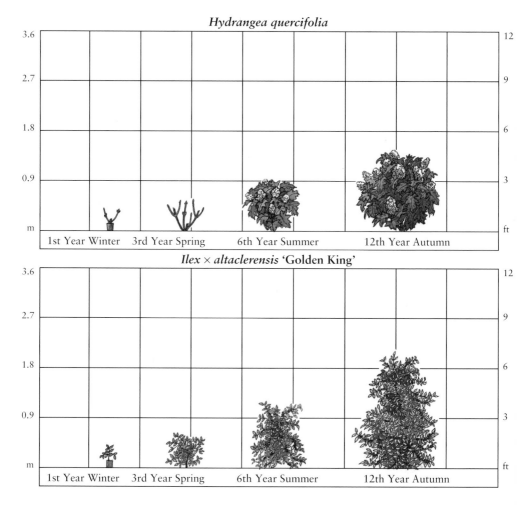

Hydrangea quercifolia

| 1st Year Winter | 3rd Year Spring | 6th Year Summer | 12th Year Autumn |

Ilex × *altaclerensis* 'Golden King'

| 1st Year Winter | 3rd Year Spring | 6th Year Summer | 12th Year Autumn |

Hydrangea quercifolia

Oak-leaf hydrangea

A slow-growing shrub, reaching 4ft by 3ft (1.2m × 90cm) in ten years. The oak-like leaves are 8in (20cm) long and can be orange, crimson or purple in the autumn. Plentiful white flowers bloom in conical panicles from late summer well into the autumn. The most spectacular hydrangea is the summer-flowering **H. paniculata** 'Grandiflora' which makes a specimen 6½ft by 6ft (2 × 1.8m). The enormous panicles of creamy-white flowers age to pink. Hydrangeas like rich, moist soils but will tolerate dry conditions.

z 5-9 shade u.h. 6ft (1.8m) ▲

Ilex × *altaclerensis* 'Golden King'

This hybrid holly makes a bush 6ft by 4ft (1.8 × 1.2m) in ten years with golden-yellow variegated, fairly spiny leaves and large red berries. Like English holly, **I. aquifolium**, it thrives best in well-drained, light soils but tolerates most soil types, shade and sun, as well as salt and atmospheric pollution. The North American species require acid soils and cold, dry winters and hot summers. They include the deciduous **I. verticillata** (z 4-8), notably the cultivar 'Christmas Cheer', and the blue hollies, **I. × merserveae** 'Blue Princess' and 'Blue Stallion' (z 4-9).

z 7-9 shade u.h. 18ft (5.4m) ▲

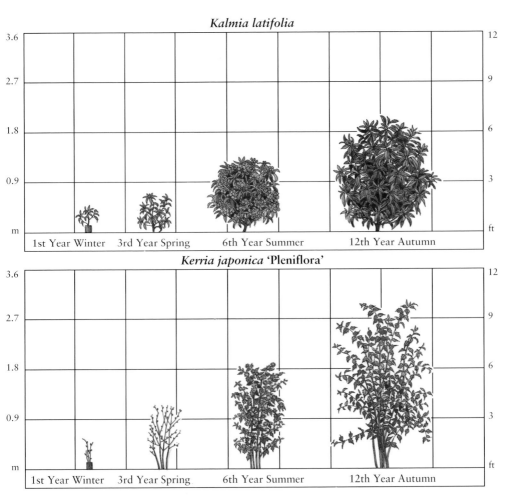

Kalmia latifolia

Calico bush or mountain laurel
This evergreen shrub requires the same moist, acid conditions as rhododendrons. It makes a rounded plant 6ft by 5ft (1.8 × 1.5m) in ten years. The shiny green, narrow oval leaves are 2 to 4in (5-10cm) long. In early summer they make a superb backdrop to the pale pink buds, which open into five-sided, bell-shaped, light pink flowers that last for several weeks.

z 4-8 sun or partial shade u.h. 10ft (3m) ▲

Kerria japonica 'Pleniflora'

This double form of kerria makes a rather stiff, upright shrub 6½ to 10ft (2-3m) tall by 6ft (1.8m) wide in ten years. The many-petaled spring flowers are deep golden yellow. The numerous suckers and green stems should be cut down soon after flowering to reduce the bulk and to give space for the next season's flowering stems. The more attractive, less commonly grown single form is less vigorous, reaching 6ft by 5ft (1.8 × 1.5m) in ten years. It has clear yellow, five-petaled open flowers. Kerrias prefer soil that is not too dry.

z 4-9 sun or shade u.h. 10ft (3m) ●

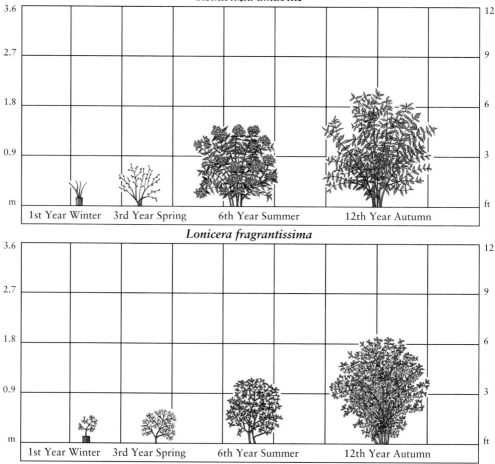

Kolkwitzia amabilis

Beauty bush

This reliable shrub is covered in bell-shaped pink flowers with a yellow throat in early summer. It is elegantly vase-shaped, the stems reaching 6ft (1.8m) or more in ten years. Peeling brown bark adds winter interest. In milder areas (z 5) **Weigela florida** is a suitable alternative, with similar summer flowers. The cultivar **'Foliis Purpureis'** has dark purple foliage and is most slow-growing, reaching 4ft (1.2m) in ten years; **'Variegata'** has cream variegated foliage and makes a dense 5ft (1.5m) bush in ten years.

z 4-8 sun u.h. 7-10ft (2.1-3m) ●

Lonicera fragrantissima

Winter-flowering honeysuckle

The small size and insignificance of the flowers of this plant are more than compensated for by the scent they exude during the coldest months of the year. This semi-evergreen species, which is often confused with the deciduous **L. standishii** and their hybrid **L. × purpusii**, makes a sparse open shrub to 6ft (1.8m) in ten years. Pale green leathery oval leaves some 2in (5cm) long follow the flowers. Although it will grow in deep shade it requires reasonably long, warm summers to ripen the flowering wood.

z (5)6-9 sun or shade u.h. 8ft (2.4cm) ▲

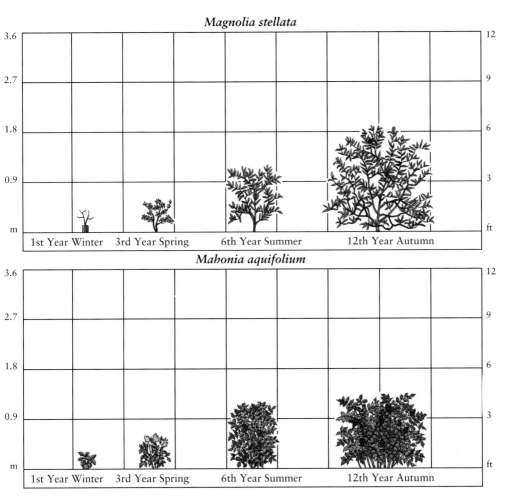

Magnolia stellata

Mahonia aquifolium

Magnolia stellata

This magnolia is popular for its sweetly scented white flowers, produced freely even when the tree is only a few years old. It grows slowly to 4ft by 4ft (1.2 × 1.2m) in ten years, making an open, sparsely branched specimen. The furry gray winter buds open in spring, before the leaves appear, into star-shaped flowers with 12 or more narrow petals. A few buds may suffer damage from late frosts. Unlike many magnolias this species is tolerant of lime, although in an alkaline soil it does benefit from the addition of peat at planting. It is tolerant of pollution.

z 5-9 sun or shade u.h. 10ft (3m) ▲

Mahonia aquifolium

This evergreen suckering shrub has an architectural quality all year round. It will reach 2ft (60cm) in height and 4ft (1.2m) in spread in less than ten years. The 1ft (30cm) pinnate leaves have up to nine spiny leaflets and change from metallic green to bronze-red in the autumn. Fragrant yellow spring flowers are followed by bunches of blue berries in summer. **M. × *media* 'Charity'** is taller and more robust, with longer leaves and tall panicles of flowers throughout the winter. Mahonias need well-drained soil.

z 5-8 shade u.h. 3-6ft (90cm-1.8m) ▲

69

Osmanthus delavayi

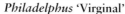

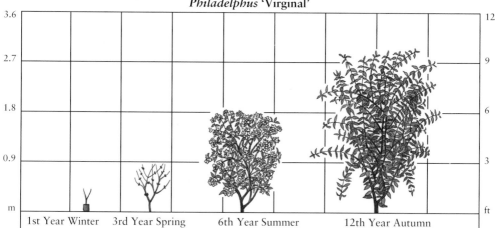

| 1st Year Winter | 3rd Year Spring | 6th Year Summer | 12th Year Autumn |

Philadelphus 'Virginal'

| 1st Year Winter | 3rd Year Spring | 6th Year Summer | 12th Year Autumn |

Osmanthus delavayi

This graceful evergreen shrub is rather tender and needs sheltered conditions and well-drained soil where it will grow slowly to 5ft by 4ft (1.5 × 1.2m) in ten years. It has small, leathery oval leaves a little over 1in (2.5cm) long, fringed with a rim of minute teeth. The sweetly fragrant flowers are creamy-white in color, shaped like tiny ½in (1.2cm) trumpets. It makes a useful hedge and should be trimmed immediately after flowering.

z 6-9 sun or partial shade u.h. 6½ft (2m) ▲

Philadelphus 'Virginal'

Virginal mock orange

This shrub presents a spectacular early summer display of scented white flowers. 'Virginal' (with **'Minnesota Snowflake'**) is among the hardiest and grows to 10ft by 5ft (3 × 1.5m) in ten years. It has 4in (10cm) leaves and large clusters of semi-double pure white flowers. **'Belle Etoile'** reaches only 5 to 6ft (1.5-1.8m) and is quite hardy. It has single white flowers, flushed pink at the base, with yellow stamens. The golden variegated *P. coronarius* **'Aureus'**, 4 ft by 3ft (1.2m × 90cm), is particularly shade-tolerant.

z 5-8 sun or light shade u.h. 10ft (3m) ●

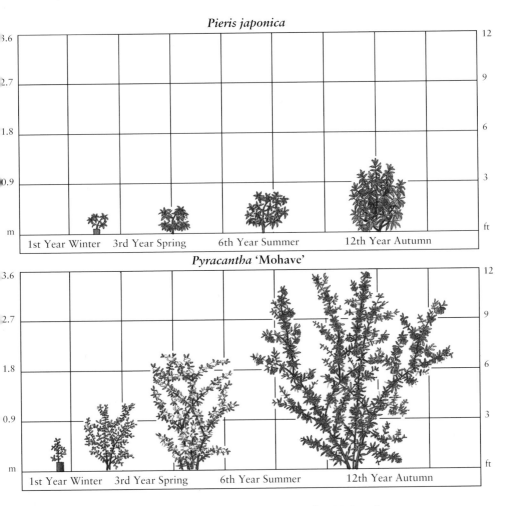

Pieris japonica

1st Year Winter	3rd Year Spring	6th Year Summer	12th Year Autumn

Pyracantha 'Mohave'

1st Year Winter	3rd Year Spring	6th Year Summer	12th Year Autumn

Pieris japonica

This beautiful evergreen plant forms a compact, bushy shrub, 4ft (1.2m) high, in ten years. The leaves emerge in spring in shades of pink, and later turn a glossy dark green. The foliage of the cultivar **'Bert Chandler'** opens salmon-pink and turns cream, white and then green, while **'Red Mill'** has bright red young foliage that turns mahogany and then dark green. The long-lasting, drooping panicles of urn-shaped white or pink flowers open from late spring to early summer. Pieris need moist, acid soils and protection from cold winds and early frosts.

z 5-9 shade u.h. 10ft (3m) ▲

Pyracantha 'Mohave'

A stiff shrub (evergreen in all but the coldest climates) which has an upright vase shape as a freestanding specimen but can also be trained against a wall. It will reach 6½ft (2m) in ten years and has small, shiny, dark green leaves. Small white flowers cover the plant in early summer and are followed by orange berries in autumn that last well into the winter, birds permitting. It is resistant to scab and fireblight diseases. *P. rogersiana* **'Flava'** has yellow berries.

z 5-10 sun and shade u.h. 16ft (5m) ▲

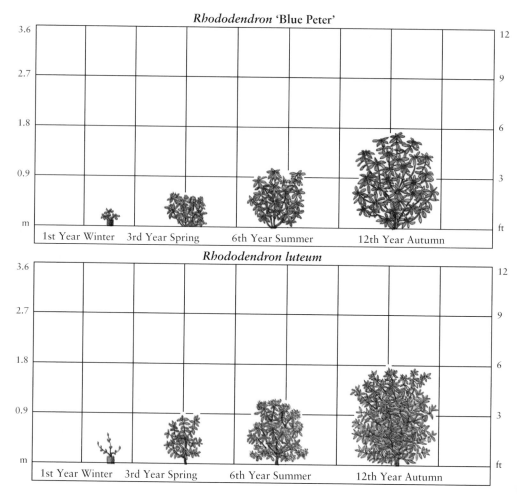

Rhododendron 'Blue Peter'

Rhododendron 'Blue Peter'
3.6 — 2.7 — 1.8 — 0.9 — m / 12 — 9 — 6 — 3 — ft
1st Year Winter   3rd Year Spring   6th Year Summer   12th Year Autumn

Rhododendron luteum
3.6 — 2.7 — 1.8 — 0.9 — m / 12 — 9 — 6 — 3 — ft
1st Year Winter   3rd Year Spring   6th Year Summer   12th Year Autumn

Rhododendron 'Blue Peter'

This evergreen rhododendron grows to 6ft (1.8m) or less, with a spread of 4 to 5ft (1.2-1.5m) in ten years. The dark glossy green foliage is a foil for the great trusses of large frilled flowers, in shades of purple, cobalt-violet and white. Each trumpet has a dark, dappled eye. *Rh. yakushimanum* hybrids (z 4-8) are very slow growing, reaching 3 or 4ft (90cm-1.2m) in ten years. Narrow leaves, with light brown felty undersides, are coupled with large white, pink, red and yellow flowers. They require humus-rich, well-drained but moisture-retentive acid soils.

z 5-8 shade u.h. 5-6ft (1.5-1.8m) ▲

Rhododendron luteum

This rhododendron, which used to be called *Azalea pontica*, is unusual in that it tolerates drier and poorer conditions than most other deciduous azaleas. It makes an open twiggy shrub up to 5ft by 5ft (1.5 × 1.5m) in ten years. In late spring and early summer trumpet-shaped yellow flowers (from pale to deep egg yolk) fill the air with their sweet scent. In autumn the leaves, which follow the flowers, turn red and orange. The hybrid deciduous azalea '**Gibraltar**' (z 5-8) has coppery-red scented flowers with fringed petals, borne in large trusses. It is a strong grower.

z 5-9 partial shade u.h. 8ft (2.4m) ▲

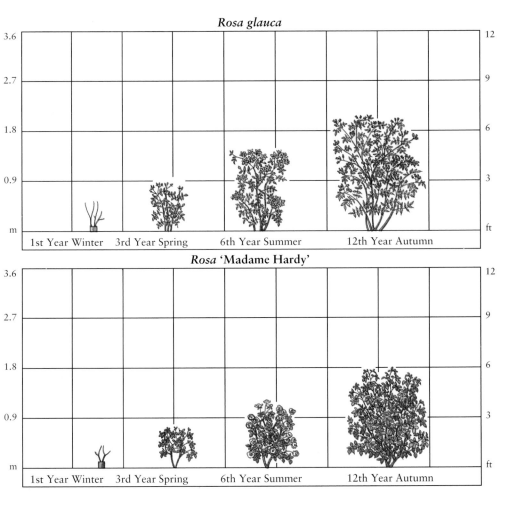

Rosa glauca

3.6 | | | | 12
2.7 | | | | 9
1.8 | | | | 6
0.9 | | | | 3
m | | | | ft

1st Year Winter   3rd Year Spring   6th Year Summer   12th Year Autumn

Rosa 'Madame Hardy'

3.6 | | | | 12
2.7 | | | | 9
1.8 | | | | 6
0.9 | | | | 3
m | | | | ft

1st Year Winter   3rd Year Spring   6th Year Summer   12th Year Autumn

Rosa glauca

Still often referred to by its old name, *R. rubrifolia*, this graceful shrub reaches 7ft (2.1m) tall, with long stems and an open vase shape. It is grown chiefly for its light blue-gray foliage. In early summer it displays single white-centered blue-pink flowers which harmonize with the foliage. These are followed by a crop of deep red-brown hips. Like many species roses, *R. glauca* thrives in any garden soil.

z 4-9 sun or partial shade u.h. 7ft (2.1m) ■

Rosa 'Madame Hardy'

A vigorous damask rose that reaches about 5ft (1.5m) tall in ten years or less. It has clear soft green foliage and a beautiful first crop of double flowers. These make perfect circles of overlapping pure white petals with a green eye. The delicious, fresh fragrance fills the air in early summer with a hint of lemon. Repeat blooms are single flowers. Many easy-to-grow hardy shrub roses are available such as 'Gertrude Jekyll' (pink), 'William Shakespeare' (crimson aging to purple) and 'Graham Thomas' (yellow).

z 4-10 sun u.h. 4-6ft (1.2-1.8m) ■

73

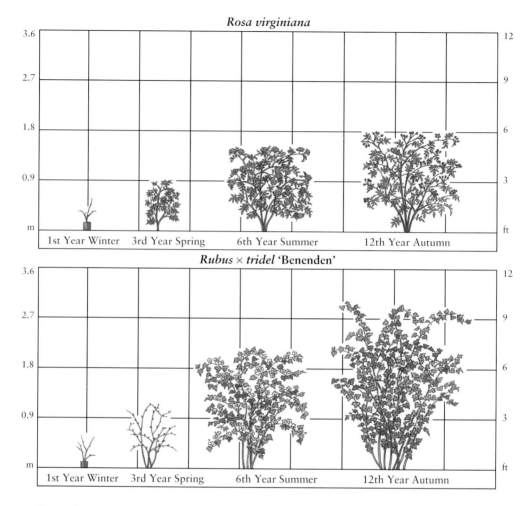

Rosa virginiana

This bush reaches 6ft (1.8m) or more in less than ten years. It has fierce, curved thorns at the base of the pinnate leaves which are bronzy when young, bright green in summer and a vibrant shade of orange in the autumn, complementing the bright red, round hips. The few clear pink single flowers open in mid-summer and are slightly scented. **R. sericea** var. **pteracantha** is grown primarily for its large orange-red thorns that look translucent and are particularly striking in winter. It has fern-like leaflets, small white four-petaled flowers and black hips.

z 4-8 sun u.h. 6½ft (2m) ■

Rubus × *tridel* 'Benenden'

This deciduous shrub has gracefully arching, thornless, reddish canes that can grow up to 6ft (1.8m) each year once the plant is established. The lobed blackberry-like leaves are nearly 4in (10cm) long. Numerous single pure white flowers are a full 2in (5cm) wide and have yellow stamens and a faint scent. The species **R. cockburnianus** has strong white stems that make it most attractive all year round. The pale green leaves are downy white underneath; purple flowers are followed by black fruit.

z 5-9 sun or partial shade u.h. 13ft (4m) ●

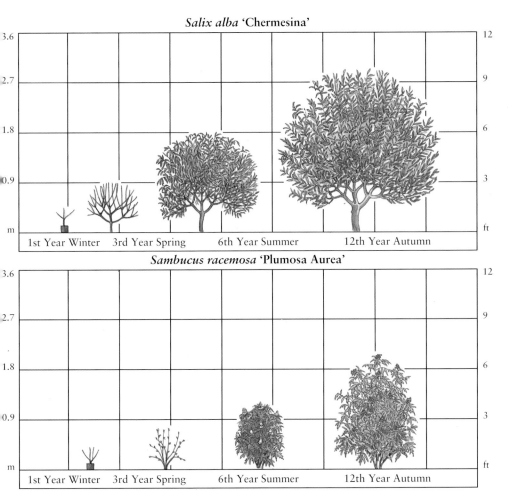

Salix alba 'Chermesina'

3.6   12

2.7   9

1.8   6

0.9   3

m   ft

1st Year Winter   3rd Year Spring   6th Year Summer   12th Year Autumn

Sambucus racemosa 'Plumosa Aurea'

3.6   12

2.7   9

1.8   6

0.9   3

m   ft

1st Year Winter   3rd Year Spring   6th Year Summer   12th Year Autumn

Salix alba 'Chermesina'

Scarlet willow

Also known as 'Britzensis', this evergreen
shrub is grown for its bright orange-red
young winter twigs. For best results,
prune it hard in spring, at least every two
years, creating a narrow upright shrub 6ft
(1.8m) or more tall in ten years. The
narrow leaves are pale green. 'Vitellina'
(golden willow) has bright yellow stems.
Some dogwoods are also grown for their
winter stems: *Cornus alba* has dark red
stems, **'Sibirica'** and *C. stolonifera*
'Flaviramea' have yellow stems; these
reach 5ft (1.5m) in ten years.

z 3-9 sun or shade u.h. 8ft (2.4m) ◆

Sambucus racemosa 'Plumosa Aurea'

This golden cut-leaf elder is among the
best yellow-leaved shrubs to illuminate a
dark corner. It is a strong grower of a
fairly upright habit, reaching 6½ft (2m) in
height and 4ft (1.2m) in width in ten
years. The dissected foliage is fern-like
and the late-spring panicles of white
flowers are followed in autumn by great
bunches of translucent red berries. Like
all elders it will grow in any soil.

z 4-7 partial shade u.h. 13ft (4m) ◆

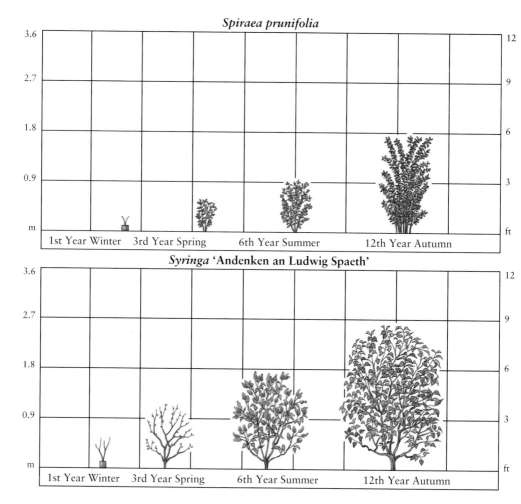

Spiraea prunifolia

3.6								12
2.7								9
1.8								6
0.9								3
m								ft

1st Year Winter   3rd Year Spring   6th Year Summer   12th Year Autumn

Syringa 'Andenken an Ludwig Spaeth'

3.6								12
2.7								9
1.8								6
0.9								3
m								ft

1st Year Winter   3rd Year Spring   6th Year Summer   12th Year Autumn

Spiraea prunifolia

This deciduous shrub has upright stems that make a narrow vase shape, 6ft by 3ft (1.8m × 90cm). The toothed oval leaves are 2in (5cm) long, shiny above and downy underneath. Pale green in summer, they turn deep red in autumn. Clusters of white button-like double flowers weigh the branches down in summer and last several weeks. *S. nipponica* 'Snowmound' is slower growing with a rounded form, covered in white flowers in early summer. *S. japonica* 'Anthony Waterer' has panicles of pink flowers in mid-summer. *S. japonica* 'Goldflame' has yellow leaves.

z 4-9 sun or partial shade u.h. 6ft (1.8m) ●

Syringa vulgaris

The lilacs make such a bold splash of color in summer, filling the air with scent, that no garden should be without one. The different cultivars of *S. vulgaris* can reach between 5ft (1.5m) and 10ft (3m) in ten years, but there are some smaller species, such as *S. meyeri* 'Palibin', that only grow to 4ft (1.2m). The best lilacs have great trusses of flowers in shades of white, cream, purple, mauve or pink. To give their best they need moisture-retentive, humus-rich soil and should not be allowed to become too congested.

z 3-7 sun u.h. 10-20ft (3-6m) ▲

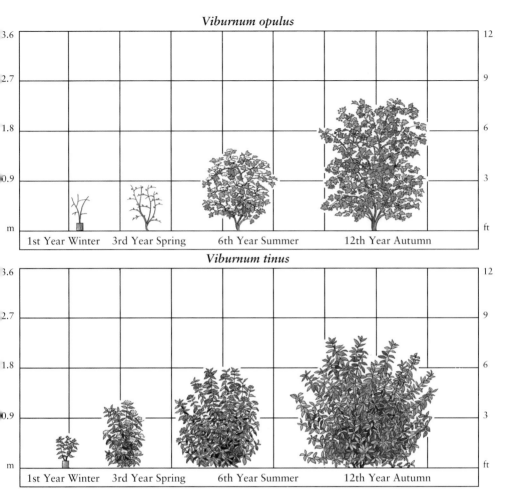

Viburnum opulus

Guelder rose

This vigorous shrub can reach 8ft (2.4m) in ten years. In summer it has white corymbs of fertile florets amid larger sterile flowers that are followed in early autumn by large bunches of translucent red berries. Cultivars include **'Roseum'**, the snowball tree, which has large inflorescences of infertile white florets; **'Compactum'** is a neater, less vigorous form, reaching 3ft (90cm) in ten years; **'Aureum'** has golden leaves all year; **'Fructo-luteo'** and **'Xanthocarpum'** have yellow fruit.

z 3-8 sun u.h. 6½-13ft (2-4m) ▲

Viburnum tinus

This versatile evergreen is resistant to atmospheric pollution and salt spray, reaching 10ft (3m) in ten years. Flattened cymes of white flowers (pink in bud) bloom from late autumn to mid-spring; the blue fruits, that ripen to black, often overlap with the flowers. The glossy foliage is dark green. **'Eve Price'** has a dense compact habit, smaller leaves and pale pink flowers (deeper pink in bud). The deciduous winter-flowering *V. × bodnantense* **'Dawn'** does well in colder climates. It has pale pink flowers, gaunt, upright stems and golden autumn foliage.

z 8-10 sun or shade u.h. 23ft (7m) ▲

Left: The large-flowered hybrid *Clematis* 'Ville de Lyon' flowers throughout the summer, growing up to 10ft (3m) each season. It flowers on the current season's growth and requires hard pruning in early spring.

Climbers

Right: *Ficus pumila* is a tender, evergreen climber that attaches itself by aerial roots, growing to 25ft (7.5m) in warm climates. Here it hugs a boundary wall, highlighting the recesses; such a use would require regular clipping, to prevent the plant overstepping its space. At the base of the wall is an edging of lilyturf (*Liriope spicata*).

Speed of growth is the greatest asset of many climbers. This quality can be used to create quick, attractive effects, introducing a vertical element on a bare wall or a trellis screen. Rapid growth can also be the worst attribute of a climber, causing it to swamp other plants, develop into a tangled mess, break structures, clog gutters or lift tiles. Less vigorous species can be slow to establish and are disappointing for their lack of early impact; nonetheless, some of the most beautiful plants are slow-growers.

There are four basic categories of climbers, distinguished by the way the plants attach themselves to their support. The secret of success lies in knowing a plant's category and its rate of growth, and managing both by using the correct means of support and careful pruning, to curtail or encourage growth as necessary.

The largest group of climbers consists of the species that twine their main stems around the support. Some twine counterclockwise, others clockwise, according to a genetic characteristic associated with the species. For example, *Wisteria sinensis*, *Ipomoea tricolor* and *Ceropegia saandersonii* twine counterclockwise and *W. floribunda*, *Lonicera periclymenum* and *Manettia inflata* twine clockwise.

The best supports for twining climbers are either trellis and wrought-iron structures or other larger plants which will not be swamped by the climber. Wires may be used, but they tend to cut through the winding stems. Pergolas, arcades, porches, summer houses and trees are all suitable structures for twining climbers.

Climbers that attach themselves by means of tendrils form the second group. Tendrils are specially adapted, flexible stalks that wave about in the air until they encounter a suitable support around which to coil. This group includes plants with simple tendrils, as in grape vines, and leaf tendrils, which

Left: The hardy, vigorous, twining climber *Wisteria sinensis* grows to 28ft (8.4m) or more. It can be trained against a building or over a pergola, making a stunning effect in early summer when it is in full flower. To achieve the best effect, the climber needs to be pruned at least once if not several times after flowering. The long fronds should be removed. It should be cut back again during winter, to two buds. 'Alba' is a white form while 'Black Dragon' has racemes of scented, double, dark purple flowers. These varieties reach a similar height to the species. 'Prolific' is much more vigorous, growing to 100ft (30m). It has single lilac flowers carried in longer racemes.

Left: The large-leaved variegated ivy *Hedera colchica* 'Sulphur Heart' (Paddy's pride) is a self-clinging climber. Here it successfully supports a *Parthenocissus henryana* which attaches itself by means of tendrils. Both are vigorous, spreading or climbing to 30ft (10m) or so.

form part of the leaves (used by *Bignonia, Cobaea, Eccremocarpus* and *Lathyrus*). More rare are flower tendrils, hook-like offshoots from the top of flower stalks (found on *Cardiospermum* and *Antigonon leptopus*), and petiole tendrils, where the leaf petiole twists itself around the support (for example, *Clematis, Asarina* and *Tropaeolum*).

The support for these climbers must be fine enough for the tendrils to embrace. Wires, strings or pig or chicken wire are suitable. These should be attached to a wall, leaving a gap of ½in (1cm) to allow the tendrils to insinuate themselves. Less vigorous species, such as *Clematis* and *Tropaeolum*, can be trained through large shrubs and other climbers, thereby extending the season of interest of the host plants.

Thirdly, there are the self-clinging climbers. Some species, such as ivies

and *Hydrangea petiolaris*, attach themselves to their support by means of a multitude of short aerial roots; others, like the Boston ivy (*Parthenocissus tricuspidata*), effectively attach themselves with sticky suckers that form on the ends of tendrils.

Self-clinging climbers provide very useful camouflage for unsightly structures. It is often suggested that they damage walls, but aerial roots are very short and scarcely penetrate the surface. Provided that the wall is in good condition when the climber starts to clothe it, the plants do not accelerate its natural deterioration. On the contrary, they protect it from bad weather and pollution. No support is necessary except when the plant is establishing itself. At that time it will need guiding towards the wall. Subsequently the plant should just be pruned back to keep it within bounds and prevent it from blocking windows, doors and gutters and from swamping roofs.

Finally there are climbers that scramble. Long, fast-growing tips are thrust up in the air, pushing their way through the support where possible and quickly producing lateral stems to secure themselves. Roses, bougainvilleas and *Rubus* species hook onto the vertical surface with thorns. They often need to be secured with ties. Other scramblers, such as winter jasmine and *Plumbago auriculata*, tend to climb up on themselves, forming a terrible jumble unless they are rigorously tied to wires stretched across the wall.

Climbers have evolved to allow seeds that germinate in heavy shade to grow rapidly through other plants and reach the light. It is important to reproduce the conditions of the plant's natural habitat as closely as possible for the best results. For example, *Ficus pumila* and *Monstera deliciosa* are native to tropical rain forests and in temperate regions should be grown as conservatory and house plants. In the northeastern states of the United States the Virginia creeper scales woodland trees and can reach 90ft (27m), reaching a third of this height in ten years or so. Such vigorous growth demands a huge growing surface in cultivation; if this is not available the plant will prove a trial.

Some climbers are herbaceous, dying down completely in the winter and

growing back the following season. Others are annuals, or are tender and can be treated as annuals in temperate regions, and are particularly useful for covering an area temporarily.

A number of climbers can be used as ground cover. The best adapted are those that produce aerial roots, such as ivies, asteranthera, bignonias, some of the trailing cucurbits and *Hydrangea petiolaris*. Many creeping forms, such as *Clematis*, *Vitis* and *Parthenocissus*, will also happily scramble along the

ground if a little brushwood is laid down to stabilize their stems. The two twining bushy honeysuckles, *Lonicera japonica* 'Aureo-reticulata' and 'Halli-ana', can be similarly encouraged.

It cannot be over-emphasized how important it is for the support to be sound before planting climbers. Walls should be well pointed and painted; trellis should be of good materials and solidly erected; wires should be properly stretched and secured; host plants must be in good health. All supports must be

The modern climbing rose 'Bantry Bay' has repeat blooms that will continue to flower until the first frosts. It has excellent lateral growth, easily spreading 12ft (3.6m) and reaching 9 to 10ft (2.7-3m) in height, so is ideal for training across the front of a house or over a long, tall garden wall.

strong enough and large enough to hold the climber.

When planting a climber, remember that the support can create a rain shadow (that is, it deflects rain from the base of the plant), so it is advisable to establish the plant as quickly and as soundly as possible. To do this will require mulching with plenty of moisture-retentive organic matter such as leaf mold, well-rotted farmyard manure or peat (although the latter should be avoided, where possible, on conservation grounds). The planting hole needs to be at least a foot (30cm) away from the base of the support – perhaps a little more at the base of a wall, which may have rubble against the foundations. The hole must also be large enough to accommodate the roots comfortably; these should be spread out away from the support before filling. Cut out any weak stems, leaving two or three strong ones that can be led to the support with a small cane. It is vital that the plant receives adequate water and sufficient nutrients while it is establishing itself.

Once climbers start to grow, the most time-consuming operations in maintaining them are pruning and training. The aim is not only to encourage optimal flowering and fruiting but also to provide a strong framework and to keep the most vigorous growers within bounds. In the early stages the strongest stems should be allowed to extend to

Below: In frost-free conditions, the Chilean potato tree, *Solanum crispum* 'Glasnevin', grows vigorously to a maximum height of 20ft (6m). It is a scrambler so requires support and careful tying in during early spring.
Right: The honeysuckle *Lonicera periclymenum* requires moisture-retentive, humus-rich soil to grow strongly, twining to 22ft (7m) in height.

the desired height. Tie them in securely, but not too tightly, as they progress. Weak tips and damaged, diseased or dead shoots should be pruned back in the winter. Make cuts on lateral shoots just above plump buds that are facing in the directions desired for new growth. If the plant is getting bare at the base, one or two stems should be cut right back to the ground before growth starts in the spring. Winter is also the time to check that the support and ties are strong.

Once established, climbers that flower on the current year's wood, and those with evergreen foliage that need a "haircut", should be pruned in spring; those that flower on the previous year's wood should be pruned in summer, leaving some material to fruit if appropriate. The vigorous species will almost certainly need fine tuning throughout the growing season.

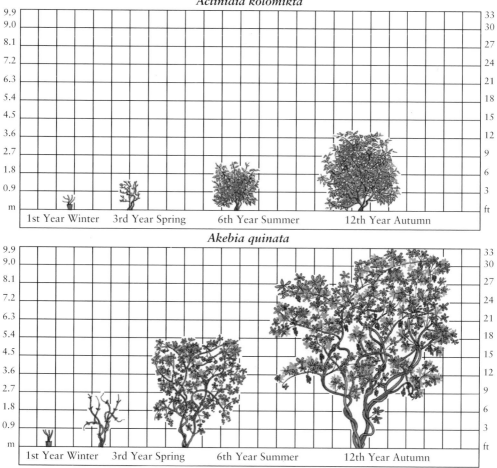

Actinidia kolomikta

1st Year Winter	3rd Year Spring	6th Year Summer	12th Year Autumn

Akebia quinata

1st Year Winter	3rd Year Spring	6th Year Summer	12th Year Autumn

Actinidia kolomikta

A hardy climber, grown for its striking variegated green, white and pink heart-shaped leaves, up to 6in (15cm) long. This twining plant reaches 10ft (3m) in ten years and needs pruning in winter to build up a strong framework. Cats are attracted to it and may destroy young plants. *A. chinensis*, the kiwi fruit or Chinese gooseberry, is less hardy (z 7) but more vigorous and has very large dull green leaves, reddish hairy stems and creamy flowers. Fruit may be produced after a hot summer. Include at least one male among female forms.

z 4 sun u.h. 14ft (4.2m) ■

Akebia quinata

A strong-growing, twining shrub which can reach 25ft (7.5m) in ten years. Hardy and evergreen in mild climates, deciduous in cold, it grows in most soils. Fragrant racemes of red to purple flowers grow on the previous season's wood from mid-spring. After a mild spring and long hot summer it produces dark purple, sausage-shaped fruits, which split to reveal black seeds and white pulpy flesh. Grow two plants from different origins to improve fruiting as clonal flowers may be sterile. Prune after flowering but leave some flowering branches if fruiting is likely.

z 4 sun or shade u.h. 40ft (12m) ●

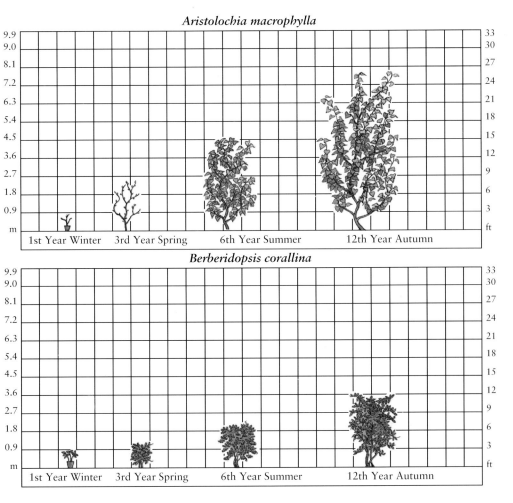

Aristolochia macrophylla

Dutchman's pipe

A vigorous deciduous climber that will reach 20ft (6m) in ten years. It gives a tropical feel to a garden, with enormous heart-shaped bright green leaves 4 to 10in (10-25cm) long. Pitcher-shaped greeny-yellow and pinky-brown pendulous flowers appear in early to mid-summer. Light pruning in late summer or early spring is necessary. The less vigorous, evergreen *A. tomentosa* grows to 6 to 10ft (1.8-3m), has dark green leaves some 2in (5cm) long and yellow to purple flowers; it requires frost-free conditions.

z 4 sun u.h. 26ft (8m) ▲

Berberidopsis corallina

Coral plant

An evergreen climber that twines its woody stems up to 12 or 15ft (3.6-4.5m) in ten years. It has thick, shiny green, spiny oval leaves which have a flat base and are up to 4in (10cm) long. The deep crimson, globular flowers are borne in hanging clusters in late summer and early autumn. The equally spectacular *Lapageria rosea* has pendent fleshy pink to red bell-shaped flowers and grows at approximately the same rate. Both come from South America and require frost-free conditions.

z 8-9 shade u.h. 16ft (5m) ▲

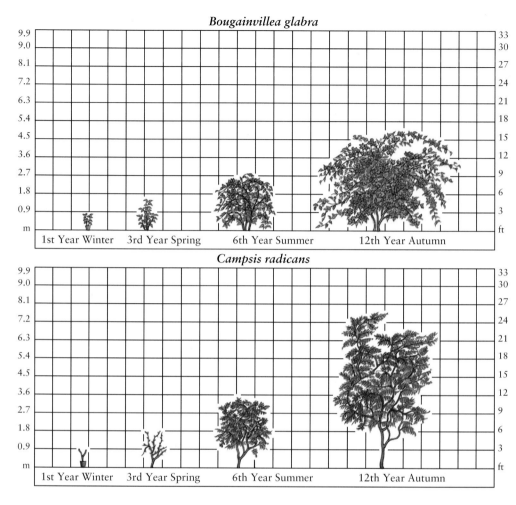

Bougainvillea glabra

This scrambler has vibrant floral bracts and is commonly seen in Mediterranean regions. It is frost tender but will grow with protection to 16ft (5m) in about ten years. Although it has hooked spines that can be ferocious, some species need tying to a support. The evergreen leaves are round to oval and the clusters of bracts which appear in summer are pinky-purple; these protect small white flowers. The cultivar 'Snow White' has white bracts with green veins and 'Magnifica' has deep reddish-purple ones. 'Variegata' has dark leaves with a creamy-white edge.

z 9   sun   u.h. 16ft (5m) ■

Campsis radicans

This wonderful exotic is hardy on a sunny wall and reaches 20ft (6m) in ten years. It is deciduous and likes most soils but needs moisture throughout the summer. The main stems cling to the wall with roots. The leaves are composed of toothed leaflets. The orange to scarlet trumpet-shaped flowers form in clusters in late summer. C. × tagliabuana 'Mme Galen' has salmon red flowers and is equally hardy. C. grandiflora has orange to pink flowers but is much less hardy. Prune in early spring after the worst frosts. Propagate using suckers.

z 4   sun   u.h. 25-40ft (7.5-12m) ■

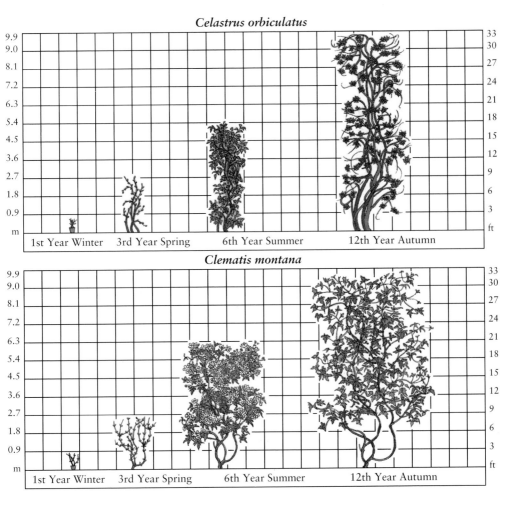

Celastrus orbiculatus

1st Year Winter 3rd Year Spring 6th Year Summer 12th Year Autumn

Clematis montana

1st Year Winter 3rd Year Spring 6th Year Summer 12th Year Autumn

Celastrus orbiculatus

Oriental bittersweet

A vigorous climber reaching 30 to 40ft (9-12m) in ten years if it scrambles up a tree, or 20ft (6m) on a shady wall. The young stems twine around a support; each stem has fierce spines either side of the first buds. The rounded leaves turn golden yellow in autumn when the yellow fruits split open to reveal bright red seeds; these persist through the winter, long after the leaves have fallen. Grow the hermaphrodite strain for successful fruiting. The hardier *C. scandens*, American bittersweet, is less invasive.

z 4 sun or shade u.h. 40-50ft (12-15m) ▲

Clematis montana

A vigorous species, it will reach 20ft (6m) in ten years, creating a thick mat of stems that are covered with creamy-white, four-petaled blooms in spring. The variety *rubens* and cultivar 'Elizabeth' have pink flowers and are more vigorous still. Some forms have a vanilla-like fragrance. Prune after flowering to prevent rampancy. *C. macropetala* is another spring-flowering species with nodding blue flowers that reaches 8ft (2.4m) in ten years. The evergreen *C. armandii* is more tender but fast-growing, reaching 20ft (6m) or more in a few years.

z 5 shade u.h. 33ft (10m) ●

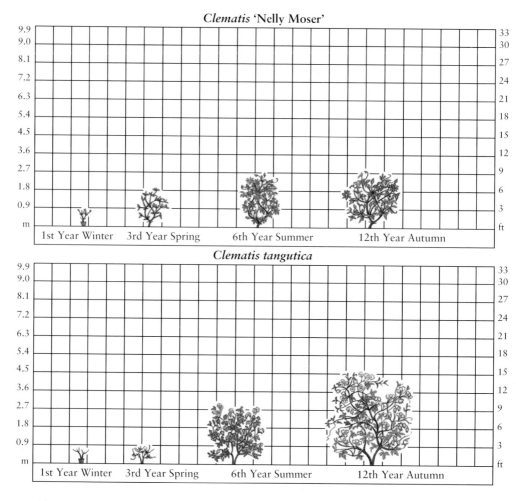

Clematis 'Nelly Moser'

9.9 / 9.0 / 8.1 / 7.2 / 6.3 / 5.4 / 4.5 / 3.6 / 2.7 / 1.8 / 0.9 / m — 33 / 30 / 27 / 24 / 21 / 18 / 15 / 12 / 9 / 6 / 3 / ft

1st Year Winter   3rd Year Spring   6th Year Summer   12th Year Autumn

Clematis tangutica

9.9 / 9.0 / 8.1 / 7.2 / 6.3 / 5.4 / 4.5 / 3.6 / 2.7 / 1.8 / 0.9 / m — 33 / 30 / 27 / 24 / 21 / 18 / 15 / 12 / 9 / 6 / 3 / ft

1st Year Winter   3rd Year Spring   6th Year Summer   12th Year Autumn

Clematis 'Nelly Moser'

A vigorous clematis growing to 8ft (2.4m) in six years. The flat flowers are 6½in (16.5cm) wide and have eight pale mauvy-pink sepals, each with a central purple bar which bleaches in the sun. Prune lightly in early spring: cut out dead vines and shorten most of the other stems to the first pair of plump buds. In a shady position cut a small number of vines right down to 1ft (30cm) to ensure plenty of renewal. Flowering can be delayed by pruning hard in early spring, making a single, slightly bigger early autumn crop of blooms instead of the usual two crops.

z 6 shade u.h. 8ft (2.4m) ■

Clematis tangutica

A late-flowering species with slender stems that will extend to 10ft (3m). The delicate foliage has a gray-blue tint that contrasts well with the nodding, four-petaled, deep yellow flowers. The silky seed tassels begin to appear before the last flowers have finished opening. It is often confused with **C. orientalis** and there are a number of selections such as **'Bill Mackenzie'** and **'Drake's Form'** which all have the same characteristic orange peel-like petals. Prune lightly in early spring.

z 5 partial shade u.h. 15-20ft (4.5-6m) ■

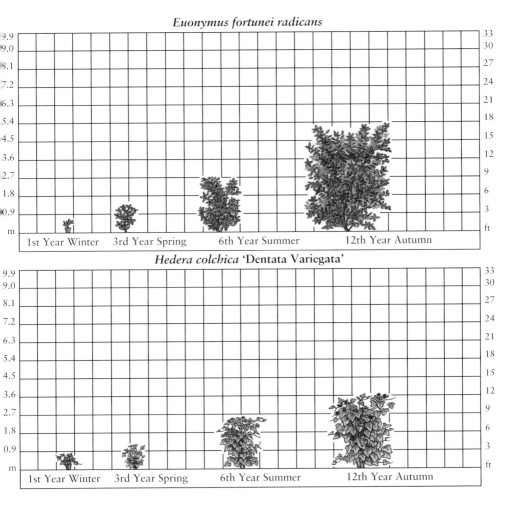

Euonymus fortunei radicans

| 1st Year Winter | 3rd Year Spring | 6th Year Summer | 12th Year Autumn |

Hedera colchica 'Dentata Variegata'

| 1st Year Winter | 3rd Year Spring | 6th Year Summer | 12th Year Autumn |

Euonymus fortunei radicans

A very hardy evergreen, which clings by aerial roots and reaches 12ft (3.6m) or more, depending on the form, in ten years. Like ivy, it has a juvenile phase in which it produces small, oval, loosely-toothed leaves. This phase lasts for as long as it continues to climb – until the supporting structure is covered or the upper height is reached. Once it stops climbing, it bears larger leaves as well as flowers and fruit. **'Variegatus'** has larger leaves with distinctive white edging and **'Colorata'** has leaves that turn reddish-purple in winter.

z 5 shade u.h. 16ft (5m) ◆

Hedera colchica 'Dentata Variegata'

This splendid ivy has the largest leaves of the genus – 6 to 8in (15-20cm) long and 4 to 5in (10-12.5cm) wide, unlobed, with rolled edges. The leathery leaves have irregular creamy-yellow margins and if crushed give off a spicy smell. En masse, they make a stunning background for autumn-berrying climbers and wall shrubs. The cultivar **'Dentata'** has equally large light green leaves, while the species has dark green ones. The leaves sometimes get burned by hard frosts but can be sheared back in early spring when growth restarts.

z 5 sun or partial shade u.h. 12ft (3.6m) ◆

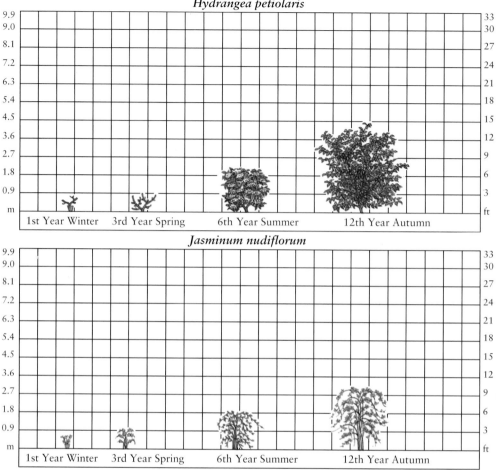

Hydrangea petiolaris

1st Year Winter	3rd Year Spring	6th Year Summer	12th Year Autumn

Jasminum nudiflorum

1st Year Winter	3rd Year Spring	6th Year Summer	12th Year Autumn

Hydrangea petiolaris

Also classified as *H. anomala petiolaris*. Slow to establish, this plant grows to 10ft (3m) in ten years, clinging by aerial roots. Flat clusters of white sterile flowers surround small cream fertile ones in early summer. The peeling, rust-colored bark is appealing in winter. Prune only to restrict. The related *Schizophragma integrifolia* (z 7) and *S. hydrangeoides* (z 5) have more open cream-colored flowers with long bracts. Both grow to 40ft (12m); *Pileostegia viburnoides* (z 7) is evergreen with fluffy flower heads and grows to half the size.

z 4 shade u.h. 50ft (15m) ▲

Jasminum nudiflorum

This is a weak scrambler reaching 9ft (2.7m) in ten years. It is often difficult to deal with; the easiest way to grow it is to allow the plant to tumble over a wall. The small oval dark green leaves appear in spring after the star-shaped yellow flowers have faded. The dark green twiggy stems should be pruned after flowering: shorten the strongest and remove weak ones, and tie the remaining stems to their support. It is very hardy but needs protection from cold winds which burn the stem tips and stop the plant from growing.

z 5 sun or shade u.h. 13ft (4m) ●

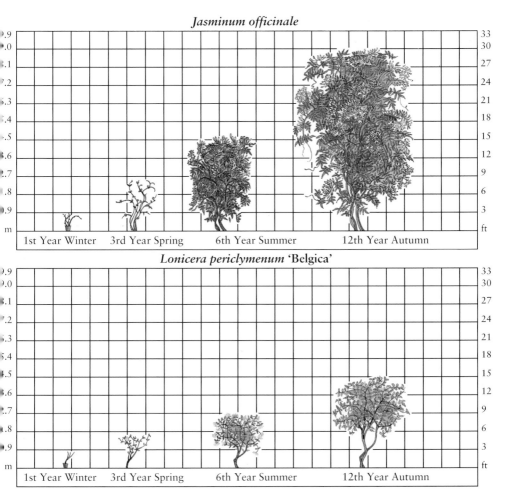

Jasminum officinale

This true climber twines its way very quickly up to 25ft (7.5m) if trained. It has delicate dark green foliage and an abundance of pink flower buds which open white throughout the summer and fill the air with a strong fragrance. It flowers best in poor soils but may need feeding to become established. The green stems need pruning in early spring to prevent them becoming tangled and leggy. *J. polyanthum* (z 9), a pure white species, needs frost-free conditions if it is to flower in late spring and early summer, or earlier if the temperature is high enough.

z 7-8 sun u.h. 42ft (12.6m) ■

Lonicera periclymenum 'Belgica'

The "early Dutch" honeysuckle will reach 13ft (4m) in ten years provided it is planted in deep, moisture-retentive soil, preferably in a well-shaded site. Stems twine over a pergola or through another climber, large shrub or tree toward the light where highly scented, cream flowers bloom from late spring to summer; these age golden yellow with rose tints on the outside. The "late Dutch" honeysuckle, 'Serotina', flowers throughout the summer and is deeper in color. Lightly prune after flowering to encourage young growth and prevent legginess.

z 4 sun u.h. 12-15ft (3.6-4.5m) ●

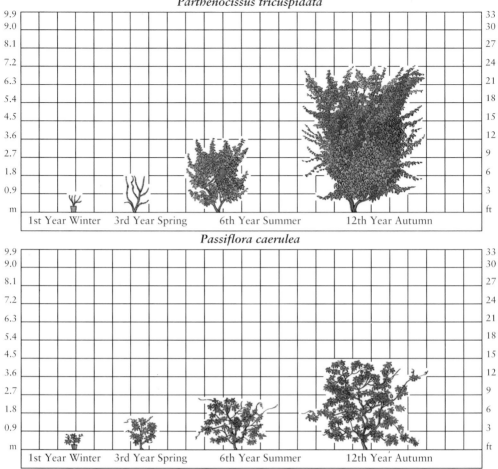

Parthenocissus tricuspidata

9.9 9.0 8.1 7.2 6.3 5.4 4.5 3.6 2.7 1.8 0.9 m
33 30 27 24 21 18 15 12 9 6 3 ft
1st Year Winter   3rd Year Spring   6th Year Summer   12th Year Autumn

Passiflora caerulea

9.9 9.0 8.1 7.2 6.3 5.4 4.5 3.6 2.7 1.8 0.9 m
33 30 27 24 21 18 15 12 9 6 3 ft
1st Year Winter   3rd Year Spring   6th Year Summer   12th Year Autumn

Parthenocissus tricuspidata

Boston ivy

This self-clinging climber will grow well almost anywhere. It is very vigorous and may become rampant in a hot summer: roots can be restricted and foliage severely pruned. The deciduous leaves, broadly lobed with toothed edges, turn bright crimson in autumn. The dark blue berries are rarely seen in cold climates. *P. quinquefolia* (z 3), Virginia creeper, is as vigorous but hardier. The related *Ampelopsis brevipedunculata*, porcelain berry, can be exceptionally invasive in warm, humid conditions.

z 4 sun or shade u.h. 65ft (19.5m) ▲

Passiflora caerulea

This passion flower is rampant in a climate with mild winters and long, hot and humid summers. In less favorable climates and well-drained soil it may be checked by frost but will grow to 12ft (3.6m) in ten years. The dark green palmate leaves are evergreen in frost-free conditions. Unusual purple and white flowers with a tiered structure appear in summer but remain closed on dull days. Yellow egg-shaped fruits follow in good years. '**Constance Elliott**' is a beautiful all-white cultivar.

z 8 sun u.h. 33ft (10m) ■

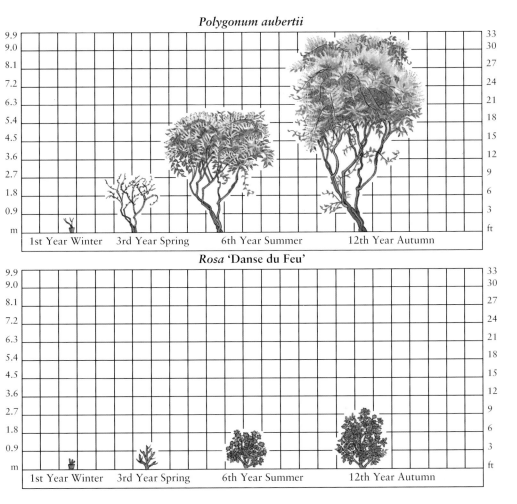

Polygonum aubertii

1st Year Winter	3rd Year Spring	6th Year Summer	12th Year Autumn

Rosa 'Danse du Feu'

1st Year Winter	3rd Year Spring	6th Year Summer	12th Year Autumn

Polygonum aubertii

This is distinguished from the true Russian vine, **P. baldschuanicum**, by the minute hairs on the stems which can be felt but rarely seen. Both grow very quickly in any soil, covering most structures in a few seasons, and reaching about 25ft (7.5m) in ten years or less. The creamy-white panicles of flowers give a frothy look throughout the summer and are followed by rust-colored seed heads. The leaves are heart-shaped. Prune at the beginning of the growing season, cutting some vines to the ground to avoid the plant becoming a tangled mass.

z 4 sun or partial shade u.h. 65ft (19.5m) ■

Rosa 'Danse du Feu'

Also known as 'Spectacular', this modern climber suits both its names. It reaches 10ft (3m) in well-drained, humus-rich, well-balanced soil. Masses of bright scarlet, slightly scented, semi-double flowers appear in early summer, with a few recurrent blooms through the summer. The foliage is, at first, bronze, turning bright glossy green in striking contrast with the flowers. Prune dead flowers and remove dead or diseased wood in late winter.

z 5 sun or partial shade u.h. 10ft (3m) ■

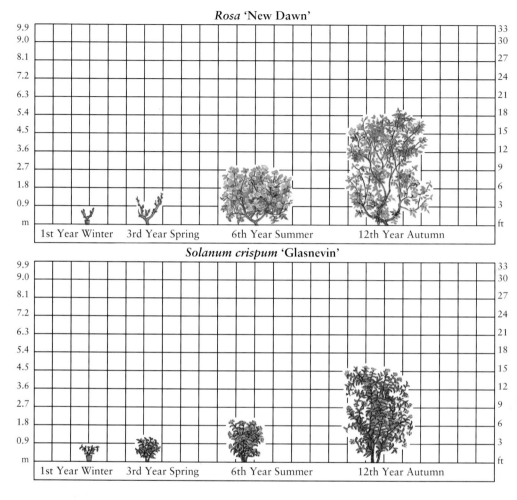

Rosa 'New Dawn'

9.9
9.0
8.1
7.2
6.3
5.4
4.5
3.6
2.7
1.8
0.9
m

33
30
27
24
21
18
15
12
9
6
3
ft

1st Year Winter   3rd Year Spring   6th Year Summer   12th Year Autumn

Solanum crispum 'Glasnevin'

9.9
9.0
8.1
7.2
6.3
5.4
4.5
3.6
2.7
1.8
0.9
m

33
30
27
24
21
18
15
12
9
6
3
ft

1st Year Winter   3rd Year Spring   6th Year Summer   12th Year Autumn

Rosa 'New Dawn'

A hardy rose, resistant to most diseases, it is suitable for shady walls, pergolas and fences. It has a vigorous, lateral habit, spreading more than 15ft (4.5m) in ten years. Leaves are a shiny light green. The flowers are apple-blossom pink with a deeper pink center and are profuse in early summer when they fill the air with a strong fragrance. There is a second flush in late summer. Prune and train to keep within bounds.

z 5 sun or partial shade u.h. 20ft (6m) ∎

Solanum crispum 'Glasnevin'

Related to the potato and tomato, this semi-evergreen scrambling climber grows strongly in a warm, sheltered position, reaching 15ft (4.5m) in ten years. It prefers well-drained, alkaline soil. The flowers are purple-blue with yellow anthers; they open between mid-summer and early autumn, followed by cream berries. The white-flowered *Solanum jasminoides* '**Album**' has twining leaf-stalks and grows to 20ft (6m) in ten years. It may produce small brown-tinted green fruit. Prune in spring after frosts; wear gloves as the plant causes a rash.

z 9 sun u.h. 20ft (6m) ∎

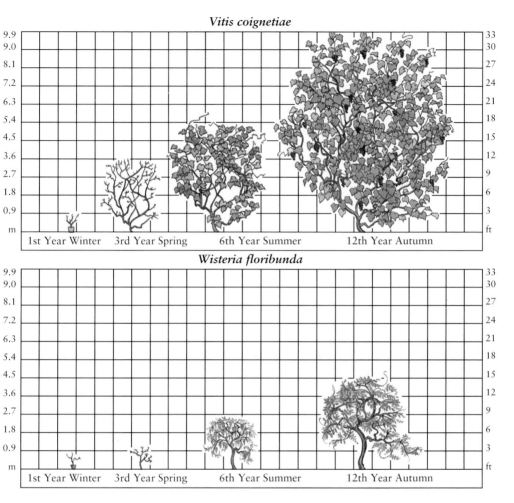

Vitis coignetiae

This grape vine reaches 30ft (9m) in ten years and will grow to a phenomenal height given the support of a tree. The leaves are broadly heart-shaped with three lobes, 8in by 4in (20 × 10cm), although they can reach 12in by 10in (30 × 25cm). In spring they are dull green with a rusty felt underside; in autumn they turn orange, red and bronze. Prune in early spring: cut back to just above a plump bud. Cultivars of **Vitis vinifera** such as '**Purpurea**' and the hybrid '**Brant**' are not as vigorous but they have equally spectacular autumn foliage. All bear fruit.

z 5 shade u.h. 75ft (22.5m) ▲

Wisteria floribunda

Japanese wisteria
This is probably hardier than the taller **W. sinensis**, which twines counter-clockwise while W. floribunda spirals clockwise. The bluey-mauve racemes of flowers of W. floribunda extend to 10in (25cm), those of W. sinensis to 3ft (1m). They are equally fragrant. Good cultivars of W. floribunda include the white '**Alba**' and pink '**Rosea**'. The long shoots need careful guiding so that they do not form a mat of twined wood. They should also be shortened in the summer to encourage flowering and again in winter.

z 4 sun u.h. 30ft (9m) ● ✳

Right: The silver variegated deadnettle *Lamium maculatum* 'Beacon Silver' has an extent of up to 3ft (90cm). It prefers a shady position, making it a most useful plant under trees, where it will colonize large areas of bare ground and suppress any weeds.

Ground cover

Left: The evergreen *Ajuga reptans* 'Atropurpurea' spreads by means of runners up to 3ft (90cm). It has attractive flowers in spring.

The characteristic common to all ground cover plants is that they are low-growing and spread quickly, forming a dense mat that smothers weeds. This makes them invaluable allies to the gardener who can use them to keep relatively large areas of the garden under control with a minimum of effort. Their attraction, however, goes far beyond the practical. Evergreen perennials, shrubs and climbers all include ground-covering plants which can form beautiful ornamental carpets that change with the seasons.

Good ground cover plants produce large quantities of leaves which cover a bare area quickly. There are many suitable species and leaves vary widely in size, shape and texture. The choice of colors is equally extensive, ranging from dark green to palest yellow-green, through metallic blue and deep maroon-red, some changing dramatically with the seasons. Variegations add greatly to the palette available, with innumerable permutations of stripes and spots. In many cases flowers and occasionally berries or seed pods add to the decorative effect of the leaves.

Ground-covering plants are a positive alternative, or complement, to grass, the ultimate ground cover. Certain ground cover plants can be used in situations where mowing would be difficult, for example, on steep banks, or where, because of shade or poor soil, grass would not grow. (For example, the shrubby *Pachysandra terminalis* and *Ruscus aeculatus* (butcher's broom), as well as the perennials *Liriope muscari* and *Iris foetidissima* (Gladwyn iris), are suitable for shady, well-drained con-

ditions.) The initial outlay is relatively low, particularly if compared to the cost of turfing (although it is more than for a bag of grass seed), and ground cover varieties are not difficult to plant.

The rates at which ground-covering plants increase depend on the type of plant selected and the suitability of the conditions. It is necessary to weed the area until the plants are well established, a task which requires considerable care, particularly with creeping ground cover, which can easily be mistaken for undesirable weeds. Subsequently, tree seedlings often germinate in the moist soil under the ground cover. These must be removed by hand. Once they are established, ground cover plants require minimal maintenance. It goes without

saying that, with a few exceptions, it is not advisable to walk on them!

For all their virtues, plants that are sold as "good for ground cover" can become a menace in the garden, and it is necessary to be on your guard to avoid problems. The main culprits are those that propagate themselves by means of stolons or rhizomes, which can spread relentlessly and swamp other small structural or ground cover plants. These invasive tendencies should be curtailed by regularly uprooting any unwanted growth during the growing season. For example, a single plant of the potentially invasive *Lamium maculatum* (spotted deadnettle) will cover a piece of ground 3ft by 3ft (90 × 90cm) in three years, anchoring itself every so often with new roots that also enable the plant to absorb additional nutrients from moist ground. By contrast, five plants of *Ajuga reptans* 'Variegata' are required to cover the same area in the same time, as is the case for the golden-leaved cultivar of *Lamium maculatum*, 'Aureum', which is significantly less vigorous than the species.

There are also variations between species of clump-forming ground cover. Six to seven plants of *Festuca glauca* are necessary to fill a 3ft (90cm) square space, but only two of *Helleborus orientalis*, which will also self-seed in the right conditions.

In all instances, coverage should be sufficiently fast to effectively overcome

Left: The lilyturf *Liriope muscari* is an evergreen perennial that makes clumps about 1ft (30cm) across, spreading by means of underground rhizomes. It requires well-drained soil in a sunny or partially shaded position.

Above: A number of evergreen or semi-evergreen sub-shrubs make good ground cover. The gray-foliaged *Senecio* 'Sunshine' and the purple-leaved sage *Salvia officinalis* 'Purpurascens' are good examples. Both like warm, sunny conditions and well-drained soil.

new weed growth, without sacrificing the characteristic habit of the plant. Each plant should barely touch its neighbor after two or three years; the ground should be completely covered after four or five years. As the foliage dies and falls it will reinforce the barrier against weeds, while providing humus for the ground cover plants.

Graham Stuart Thomas's authoritative book *Plants for Ground Cover* (J.M. Dent and Sons, London, 1990) contains a comprehensive list of genera and species; it is invaluable for guidance on planting distances and I refer to it often. Getting planting distances right is crucial. Ground cover trial plots at Bath University have demonstrated the adverse effects of dense planting to achieve a quick result. Large, unsightly patches of dead vegetation appeared as the competition between plants became too great, causing some to die. At the other extreme, sparingly planted plots also failed to fulfil their purpose. The competition from weeds was so great that the ground cover had considerable difficulty establishing itself; and as the plants spread to fill the empty spaces, they lost their identity and character, becoming leggy and unattractive.

Some of the most interesting associations of ground cover plants I have seen include: a continuous edging of lilyturf (*Liriope muscari*) around a bed of evergreen azaleas; hellebores mingling with ferns and lungwort (*Pulmonaria* spp.);

Saxifraga stolonifera threading its way beneath low clumps of box; drifts of the soft gray *Chrysanthemum haradjanii* and the round leathery maroon leaves of *Bergenia* 'Abendglut' with clumps of blue fescue (*Festuca glauca*) and brown grass *Carex buchanii*; the low-growing *Prunus laurocerasus* 'Otto Luyken' underplanted with variegated ivies. All these combinations make bold displays which last throughout the year, some changing attractively as the seasons progress.

THE GROWTH CHARTS

Plants are illustrated from above, to show their spread across an area 3ft by 3ft (90 × 90cm). Appropriate planting distances vary between species and forms.

Top left: A combination of evergreen and deciduous shrubs makes a colorful tapestry of foliage that perfectly smothers weeds. This bed contains (from the foreground back) golden spiraea, gray-leaved rue, purple berberis, spikey caryopteris and blue juniper. Such a pleasing effect can usually be achieved in three to five years.

Bottom left: The blue fescue, *Festuca glauca*, associates perfectly with border pinks.

Below: The hardy hybrid cherry laurel *Prunus laurocerasus* 'Otto Luyken' has a low-growing habit. It spreads 4 to 6ft (1.2-1.8m) and flowers in early summer.

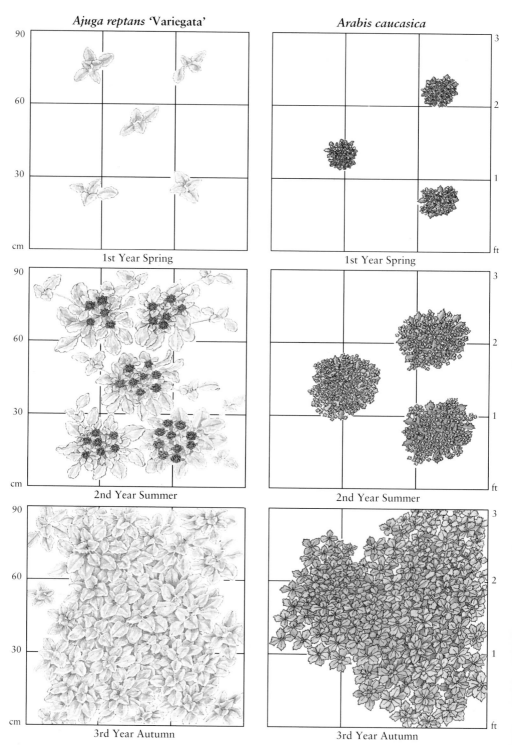

Ajuga reptans 'Variegata'

Arabis caucasica

1st Year Spring

1st Year Spring

2nd Year Summer

2nd Year Summer

3rd Year Autumn

3rd Year Autumn

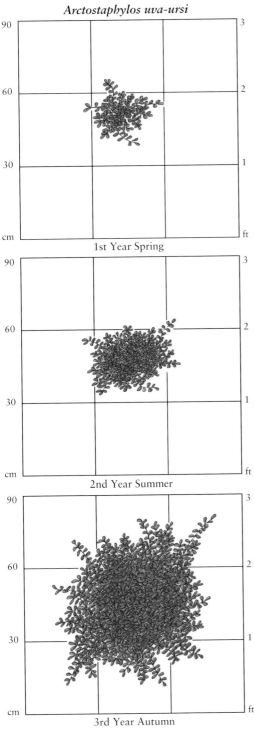

Arctostaphylos uva-ursi

90
60
30
cm ft
3
2
1
1st Year Spring

90
60
30
cm ft
3
2
1
2nd Year Summer

90
60
30
cm ft
3
2
1
3rd Year Autumn

Ajuga reptans 'Variegata'

This evergreen plant tolerates most soils and positions but its stoloniferous stems spread most rapidly in moist, lightly shaded conditions. It forms a close mat of smooth oval gray-green and white leaves, covered in spring with small spikes of blue flowers. 'Atropurpurea' has shiny, deep reddy-purple leaves, 'Multicolor' (syn. 'Rainbow') has green and bronze leaves mottled cream and edged pink and 'Jungle Beauty' has large green, rounded leaves and 15in (37.5cm) tall blue flower spikes.

z 4-9 sun or shade u.h. 4in (10cm) u.s. 1ft (30cm)

Arabis caucasica

Often listed in catalogues as *A. albida*, this useful plant forms loose mats of gray-green oblong leaves. The bright, white, slightly fragrant flowers of four petals are carried in spring in lax racemes 8in (20cm) tall. It does well in dry situations such as a sunny wall or in crevices. Dead-head after blooming to improve the appearance of the ground cover. Propagate from seed in autumn or, for the best forms such as the double 'Flore-Pleno', the pink 'Rosabelle' or the green-and-yellow leaved 'Variegata', from cuttings taken in summer.

z 3-9 sun u.h. 6in (15cm) u.s. 10in (25cm)

Arctostaphylos uva-ursi

Bearberry

This evergreen dwarf shrub makes ideal cover for a well-drained acid soil. It is scarcely 5in (12.5cm) in height and spreads to about 2ft (60cm) in four years. It is tolerant of the poorest soils and coastal conditions. Small shiny green leaves make a dense weed-smothering mat. Tiny pale pink, bell-shaped spring flowers are followed by bright red autumn berries. 'Massachusetts' is denser, lower-growing and bears quantities of flowers that last for six weeks.

z 2-8 sun or partial shade u.h. 5in (12.5cm) u.s. 2ft (60cm)

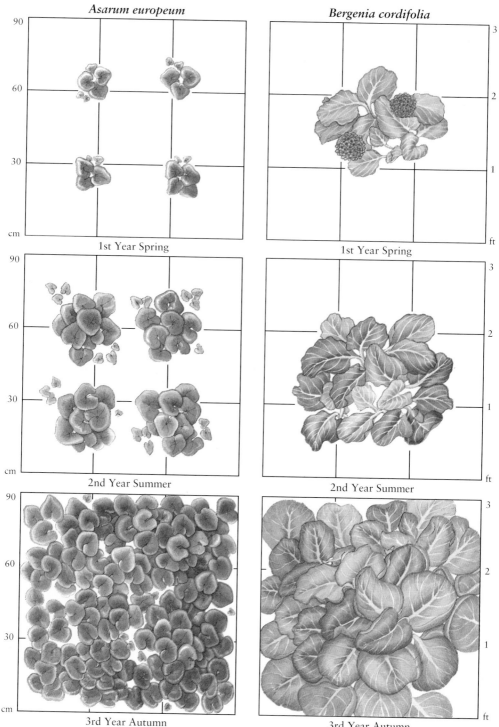

Asarum europeum

1st Year Spring

2nd Year Summer

3rd Year Autumn

Bergenia cordifolia

1st Year Spring

2nd Year Summer

3rd Year Autumn

Chiastophyllum oppositifolium

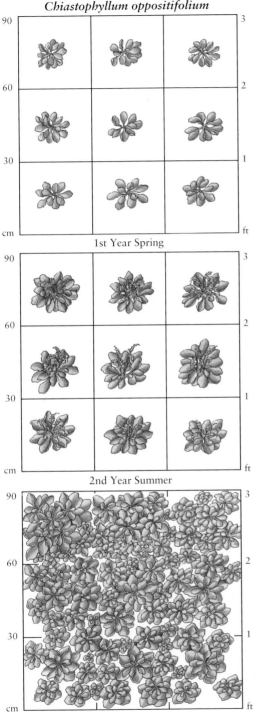

1st Year Spring

2nd Year Summer

3rd Year Autumn

Asarum europeum

European ginger

A delightful and uncommon ground cover for cool, moist conditions. It produces a carpet of evergreen rounded to kidney-shaped leaves, 1 to 4in (2.5-10cm) long, that are a bright glossy green with pale veins, creating a subtly marbled effect. The stems stand 4 to 6in (10-15cm) high. The curious maroon flowers are bell-shaped and are often hidden at ground level. This little plant is useful for rockeries, woodland areas or as an edging to a herbaceous border, spreading to 12in (30cm).

z 4-8 shade u.h. 6in (15cm) u.s. 12in (30cm)

Bergenia cordifolia

This excellent plant is evergreen in milder climates but goes a little limp in harsh winters. It has large leathery, rounded, glossy leaves with tints of red. Generous heads of lilac-pink flowers are borne on 18in (45cm) stalks in late winter or early spring. The cultivar **'Purpurea'** has striking foliage that tends to be purplish in winter, and the flowers are darker on red stems. Good alternatives include *B. purpurascens* and its cultivar 'Ballawley', and *B.* 'Abendglut', 'Morgenrote' and 'Silberlicht'.

z 4-9 sun or partial shade u.h. 16in (40cm) u.s. 2ft (60cm)

Chiastophyllum oppositifolium

Sometimes referred to as *Cotyledon oppositifolia*, this charming succulent needs well-drained soil and does best in partial shade. It forms neat rosettes of rounded to oval fleshy pale green leaves, 2 to 4 in (5-10cm) long, that have regularly serrated edges. Each clump will spread about 1ft (30cm), forming effective ground cover, and will blossom in spring and summer on 6 to 8in (15-20cm) stalks. Tiny pale yellow flowers hang in 1 to 2in (2.5-5cm) long racemes resembling catkins.

z 6(5)-9 sun or shade u.h. 8in (20cm) u.s. 1ft (30cm)

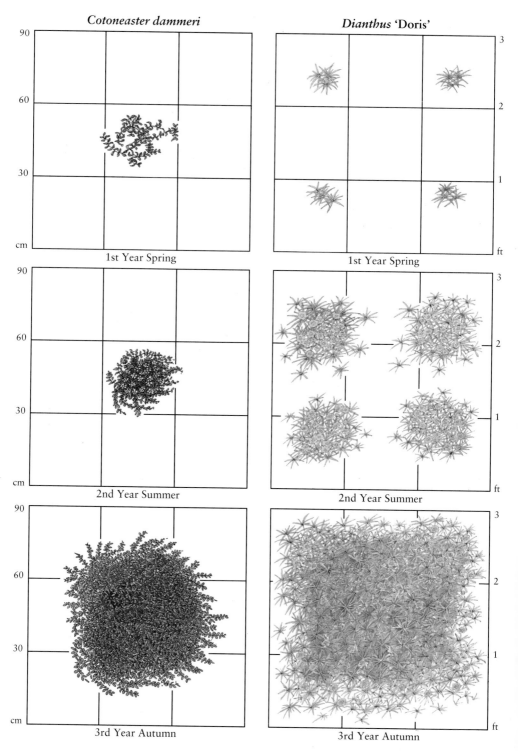

Cotoneaster dammeri

Dianthus 'Doris'

1st Year Spring

1st Year Spring

2nd Year Summer

2nd Year Summer

3rd Year Autumn

3rd Year Autumn

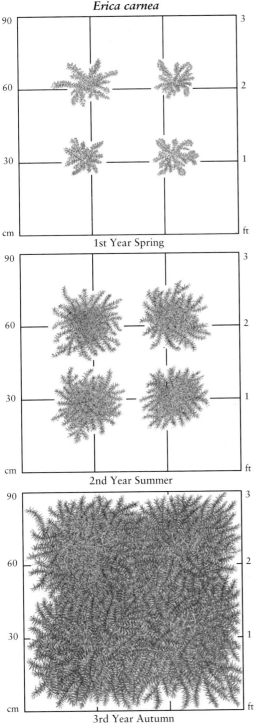

Erica carnea

90

60

30

cm — ft

1st Year Spring

90

60

30

cm — ft

2nd Year Summer

90

60

30

cm — ft

3rd Year Autumn

Cotoneaster dammeri

This carpet-forming evergreen shrub makes an ideal ground cover for a well-drained soil. The alternating oval leaves are about 1in (2.5cm) long. Small white flowers appear in late spring, followed in autumn by a rich crop of bright red berries. The cultivar 'Skogholm' is taller at 1ft (30cm) and has arching stems. *C. horizontalis* (wall-spray) also has a spreading habit and is taller still at 2ft (60cm). Its foliage is deciduous (there is also a variegated form) and it tolerates much colder, more shaded conditions.

z 6-9 sun or partial shade u.h. 4in (10cm)
u.s. 2ft (60cm)

Dianthus 'Doris'

'Doris' is just one of the many border pinks and carnations that are suitable for ground cover. They all thrive best in well-drained neutral to limy soils and like an open position, so are suited to sea- or oceanside gardens. The leaves are grass-like and vary in color from deep green to gray-green. The blossoms are mostly highly scented and range in color from white to crimson through all the shades of pink. Petals may be rounded or frilly, and often have attractive markings. 'Doris' is a vigorous modern cultivar with salmon pink flowers.

z 3-8 sun u.h. 1ft (30cm) u.s. 1ft (30cm)

Erica carnea

To thrive, heathers need a fungus that colonizes the whole plant; this fungus normally requires acid conditions, hence the need for acidic soils to grow ericas successfully. However, *E. carnea* is one of the few species that tolerate a small amount of alkaline content in the soil. It has wiry stems with minute narrow leaves (golden-tinted in 'Aurea') and is covered from late autumn to late spring with tiny urn-shaped flowers. These range in color from white to carmine through different shades of bluey-pink. Heathers should be sheared over in spring.

z 6-8 sun u.h. 9in (22.5cm) u.s. 18in (45cm)

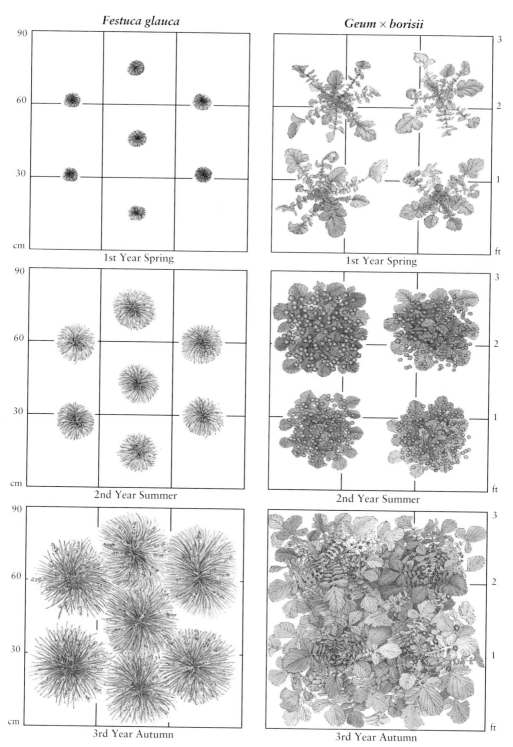

Festuca glauca

90

60

30

cm

1st Year Spring

90

60

30

cm

2nd Year Summer

90

60

30

cm

3rd Year Autumn

Geum × borisii

3

2

1

ft

1st Year Spring

3

2

1

ft

2nd Year Summer

3

2

1

ft

3rd Year Autumn

Hedera helix 'Glacier'

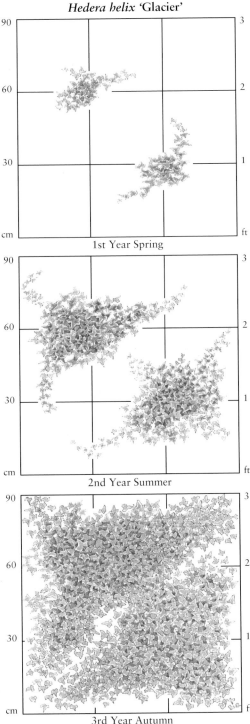

1st Year Spring

2nd Year Summer

3rd Year Autumn

Festuca glauca

This grass has characteristically gray-blue evergreen foliage that makes a neat edging or useful foil or focal plant in a border. It forms dense clumps about 6in (15cm) tall and the gray-blue flowers stand about 10in (25cm) high in summer. **'Sea Urchin'**, **'Sea Blue'**, **'Seven Seas'** and **'Silver Sea'** vary in hue and are sturdier and of more compact habit. Other grasses that give good ground cover include *Stipa calamagrostis*, *Phalaris arundinacea* **'Picta'** (gardener's garters), *Pennisetum alopecuroides*, which are all herbaceous, and the evergreen *Luzula maxima*.

z 4-9 sun u.h. 10in (25cm) u.s. 9in (22.5cm)

Geum × borisii

The bright orange-red flowers of this plant are its chief glory. They stand 9 to 12in (22.5-30cm) high and are about 1½in (4cm) across, with six petals and a bunch of orangey-yellow stamens. Flowers are produced most abundantly in late spring to early summer and then sporadically until the first frosts. The glossy green rounded pinnate foliage makes clumps about 1ft (30cm) wide. Evergreen in milder areas, it will lose its foliage in cold zones. *Geum chilense* **'Mrs Bradshaw'** is taller with deeper orange flowers and *G. rivale* has later, coppery-pink flowers.

z 5-9 sun u.h. 10in (25cm) u.s. 1ft (30cm)

Hedera helix 'Glacier'

English ivy is one of the most useful evergreen ground cover plants for shady positions. It has many different forms: **'Glacier'** has purplish stems and variegated leaves of grayish-green with patches of lighter gray and a cream margin; **'Tricolor'** has leaves with broad creamy-white margins, which are often pink in winter; **'Goldheart'** is yellow-centered; **'Atropurpurea'** is dark green, turning deep purple in winter; **'Digitata'** has narrow lobes; the bird's-foot ivy **'Pedata'** is light green to yellow, with a variegated form, **'Caenwoodiana Aurea'**.

z 5-9 shade u. h. 1in (2.5cm) u.s. 18in (45cm)

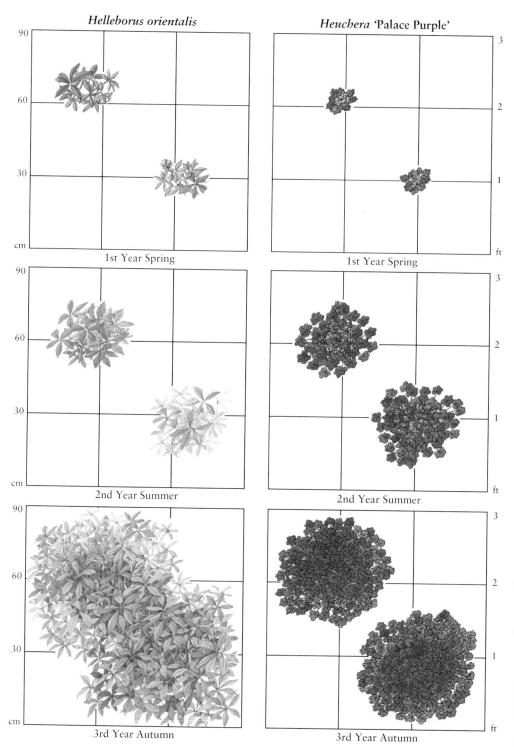

Helleborus orientalis

Heuchera 'Palace Purple'

1st Year Spring

1st Year Spring

2nd Year Summer

2nd Year Summer

3rd Year Autumn

3rd Year Autumn

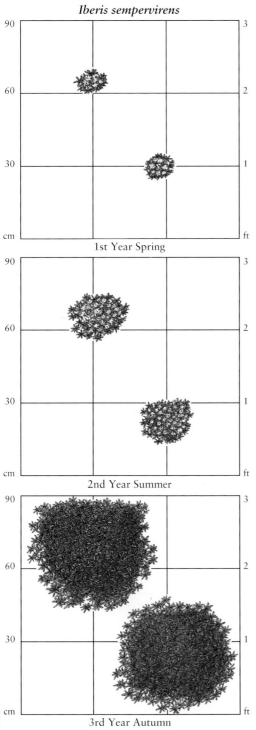

Iberis sempervirens

1st Year Spring

2nd Year Summer

3rd Year Autumn

Helleborus orientalis

The Lenten rose is a beautiful evergreen plant that self-seeds and has many variations. The bold, creamy-white to dark purple flowers with yellow stamens appear in late winter to early spring and are held 12 to 18in (30-45cm) high, above mid-green leathery leaves. It is most successful in moist soil which never dries out, with protection from wind and rain, which spoil the flowers. *H. niger*, the Christmas rose, has large white flowers tinged pink on the outside. *H. viridis* and *H. foetidu*s have green nodding flowers.

z 3-8 shade u.h. 1ft (30cm) u.s. 2ft (60cm)

Heuchera 'Palace Purple'

A good foliage plant, evergreen in mild climates but dying down in cold winters, that makes clumps of heart-shaped leaves, reddy-purple above, brighter red beneath. In early summer a delicate spray of minute bell-shaped flowers appears. Coral bells or alum root, *H. sanguinea*, is an American native that flowers abundantly in spring and sporadically throughout the growing season, particularly if dead-headed. The blossoms of the species are blood-red but there are pink and white forms. The rounded leaves are dull green.

z 4-9 sun or partial shade u.h. 18in (45cm) u.s. 18in (45cm)

Iberis sempervirens

Candytuft

This sub-shrub is frequently used as an edging or in rockeries. It forms a low, compact cushion of dark evergreen shiny leaves, smothered in pure white flowers in late spring. The plant will spread to 2ft (60cm) but is easily contained by frequent pruning. 'Snowflake' has larger-petaled flowers that seem brighter. 'Little Gem' is a smaller and more erect pink cultivar. It is best to grow all varieties in well-drained, slightly alkaline soil. Trim the flowers once they are finished. Propagate by taking cuttings in summer.

z 4-8 sun u.h. 9in (22.5cm) u.s. 2ft (60cm)

Iris foetidissima

Juniper horizontalis 'Gray Pearl'

1st Year Spring

1st Year Spring

2nd Year Summer

2nd Year Summer

3rd Year Autumn

3rd Year Autumn

Lamium maculatum

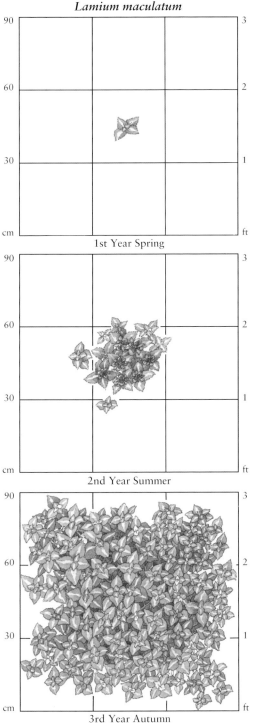

1st Year Spring

2nd Year Summer

3rd Year Autumn

Iris foetidissima

Gladwyn iris or stinking iris
A hardy iris that thrives in both dry, inhospitable soils and more fertile, moist soils. It has tall, dark green, strap-shaped leaves and discreet browny-purple flowers in early summer, followed in autumn by showy orange seed pods that last throughout the winter. *I. foetidissima citrina* has larger pale yellow flowers. **'Variegata'** is a beautiful foliage plant with creamy variegated leaves but it rarely flowers so does not produce seed pods. Like most irises these varieties produce rhizomes.

z 5-9 shade u.h. 18in (45cm) u.s. 2ft (60cm)

Juniper horizontalis 'Gray Pearl'

Of all the prostrate conifers, junipers rank among the best and most numerous. *Juniperus × media* **'Pfitzeriana'** is a hardy hybrid that will spread easily to 8ft (2.4m) and ultimately much wider, and reach a height of 5ft (1.5m) in ten years, making it a large specimen for a small garden. *J. horizontalis* is a much flatter species. Some cultivars, such as **'Emerald Spreader'**, are barely 4in (10cm) high. **'Glauca'** has bluish foliage 6in (15cm) high with a spread of 4ft (1.2m) after ten years.

z 3-9 sun or partial shade u.h. 8in (20cm)
u.s. 6-10ft (1.8-3m)

Lamium maculatum

Spotted deadnettle
This plant is useful under very shady trees and large shrubs where it is difficult to establish anything else, but it may be invasive elsewhere. The leaves have a central cream stripe. The mauvy-pink flowers blossom in early summer. Several good cultivars are less vigorous, spreading to just 1ft (30cm). **'Beacon Silver'** has silver leaves with narrow green edging and pink flowers. **'White Nancy'** is similar but with white flowers. **'Aureum'** has pale yellow leaves with a creamy white stripe and pink flowers.

z 3-9 shade u.h. 8in (20cm) u.s. 3ft (90cm)

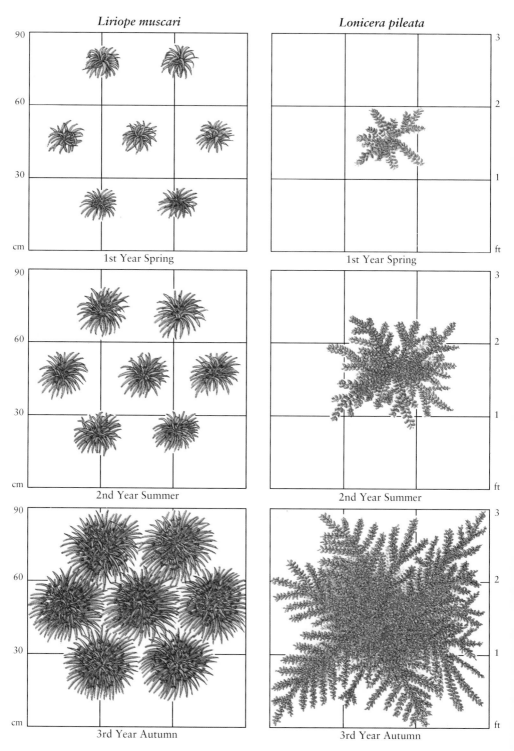

Liriope muscari

Lonicera pileata

1st Year Spring

1st Year Spring

2nd Year Summer

2nd Year Summer

3rd Year Autumn

3rd Year Autumn

Lysimachia nummularia

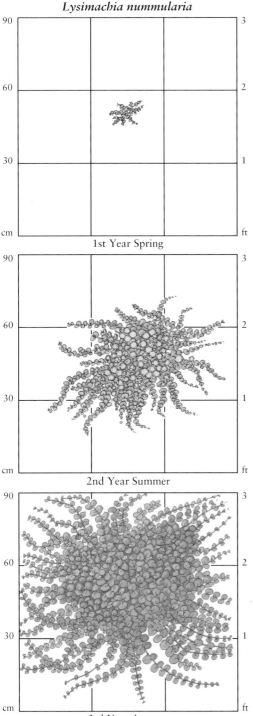

1st Year Spring

2nd Year Summer

3rd Year Autumn

Liriope muscari

This member of the lily family resembles a broad-leaved grass with evergreen clumps of dense, dark green leathery foliage that smothers weeds effectively. The dark mauve flowers appear in late summer, followed by bunches of shiny black berries that last well into winter. **'Majestic'** is a robust form. It slowly spreads by underground rhizomes and benefits from having the leaves cut right down in spring before the new growth starts. *L. spicata* is frequently seen in Italy as an edging but may be invasive.

z 6-9 sun or shade   u.h. 15in (37.5cm)
u.s. 1ft (30cm)

Lonicera pileata

The neat spreading habit of this honeysuckle makes it an ideal choice for bold plantings that require larger areas of ground cover. It has stiff branches that fan out in layers. The shiny oval leaves are just over 1in (2.5cm) long. The little white flowers are mostly hidden under the foliage and are followed by purple berries. This shrub is evergreen in all but the coldest areas. Climbing honeysuckles, such as **L. japonica** and **L. periclymenum**, can also be used as ground cover, spreading to 3 or 4ft (90cm-1.2m).

z 5-10 sun or shade u.h. 2ft (60cm)
u.s. 3ft (90cm)

Lysimachia nummularia

Creeping jenny
This vigorous spreader is rampant in moist conditions, which are necessary if the plant is grown in a sunny position. The opposite evergreen rounded leaves are just under 1in (2.5cm) long and covered in summer with bright yellow flowers. The golden form **'Aurea'** has yellow-green leaves. It is somewhat less invasive and suitable for edging. In areas where it is too invasive, plant the white sweet woodruff, **Galium odoratum**, which needs moisture and partial shade.

z 3-9 sun or partial shade u.h. 1in (2.5cm)
u.s. 2-3ft (60-90cm)

117

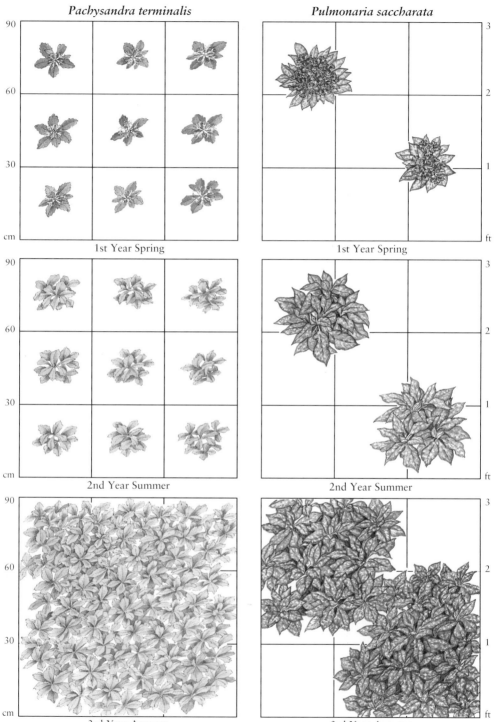

Pachysandra terminalis

Pulmonaria saccharata

1st Year Spring

1st Year Spring

2nd Year Summer

2nd Year Summer

3rd Year Autumn

3rd Year Autumn

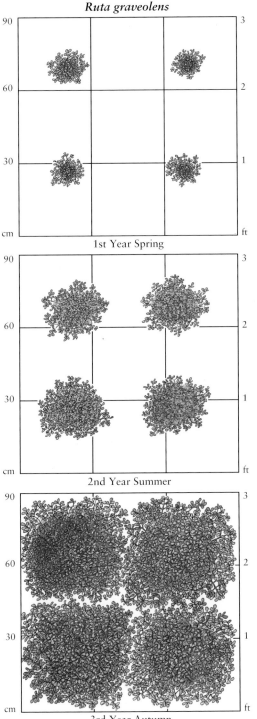

Ruta graveolens

90 — 60 — 30 — cm
1st Year Spring
3 — 2 — 1 — ft

90 — 60 — 30 — cm
2nd Year Summer
3 — 2 — 1 — ft

90 — 60 — 30 — cm
3rd Year Autumn
3 — 2 — 1 — ft

Pachysandra terminalis

One of the best ground cover plants for dense shade, pachysandra is widely grown in the United States. It has leathery shiny green toothed leaves at the top of stalks 6 to 8in (15-20cm) tall. The small creamy-white flowers appear in spring and are scented. It prefers lime-free conditions and spreads rapidly by rhizomatous roots provided there is plenty of moisture in the establishment period. There are variegated forms that are somewhat less vigorous, 'Silveredge' and 'Variegata', which have narrow white margins on their leaves.

z 4-8 shade u.h. 10in (25cm) u.s. 3ft (90cm)

Pulmonaria saccharata

Bethlehem sage
This has larger leaves and flowers than the common lungwort (*P. vulgaris*), also known as soldiers and sailors or Joseph and Mary for its pink and blue flowers. Both smother weeds with their spotted green leaves, flower early in the year and die down in cold winters. 'Argentea' has silvery-white leaves, 'Cambridge Blue' deep pink and blue flowers, 'Pink Dawn' all pink flowers and 'Sissinghurst White' white flowers. All need cool moist soil. Cut back ragged leaves.

z 3-8 shade or partial sun u.h. 9-12in (22.5-30cm) u.s. 2ft (60cm)

Ruta graveolens

Herb of grace or common rue
This old-fashioned herb is mostly grown as an ornamental. It makes mounds of gray-green dainty foliage about 18in (45cm) high. The leaves are deeply divided and somewhat ferny with a bitter smell. The small yellow flowers appear in mid-summer and continue until early autumn. Most commonly found are the superior blue-gray forms, 'Jackman's Blue' and 'Blue Beauty'. It thrives in well-drained soils and is evergreen in mild areas, but becomes rather ragged in colder climates. Trim in early spring.

z 4-9 sun u.h. 18in (45cm) u.s. 18in (45cm)

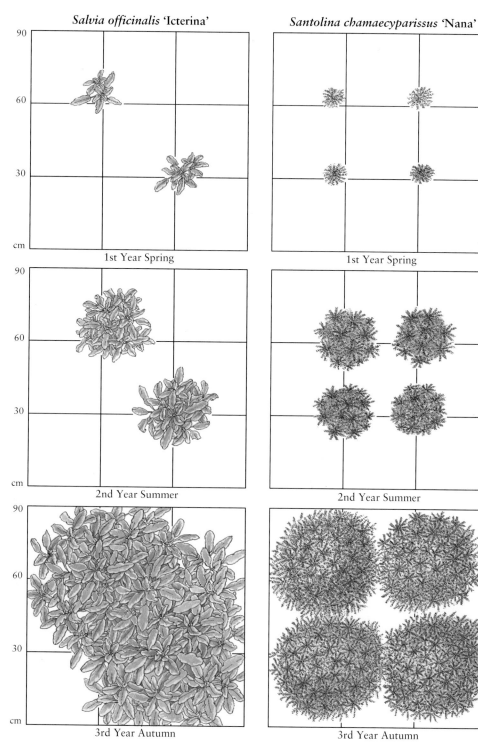

Salvia officinalis 'Icterina'

Santolina chamaecyparissus 'Nana'

1st Year Spring

1st Year Spring

2nd Year Summer

2nd Year Summer

3rd Year Autumn

3rd Year Autumn

Sarcoccoca humilis

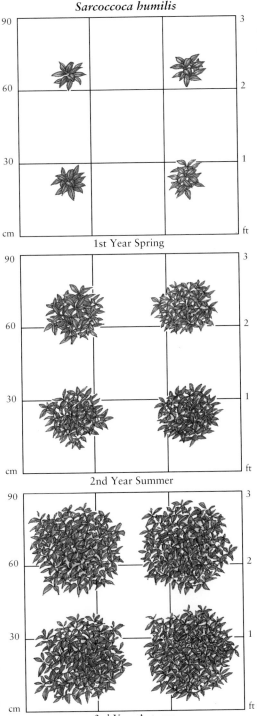

1st Year Spring

2nd Year Summer

3rd Year Autumn

Salvia officinalis 'Icterina'

This is the golden variegated form of the common culinary sage. It forms a low spreading bushy shrub that needs sharp drainage. The oval leaves are 1 to 2½in (2.5-6.5cm) long, gray-green with soft hairs in the species. 'Icterina' has yellow mottling on the leaves, **'Variegata'** white variegations, **'Purpurascens'** purple flushes and **'Tricolor'** red, green and white markings. All have light violet-blue flowers except **'Alba'** which has white flowers. It is evergreen in mild winters but dies off in harder climates. Cut back in spring to encourage bushiness.

z 3-9 sun u.h. 18in (45cm) u.s. 2ft (60cm)

Santolina chamaecyparissus 'Nana'

Cotton lavender
This plant makes good ground cover for dry, well-drained soils but it does not like cold, damp conditions. It has gray feathery aromatic foliage, gray-green in **S. virens**. A member of the daisy family, the flowers are reduced to button-like bright yellow heads without florets. **S. neapolitana** has lemon-yellow flowers. The species is vigorous, spreading to 2ft (60cm) with a height of 18in (45cm) or more, but 'Nana' is much more compact and manageable in a small space. Cut back the stems fairly hard in spring.

z 7-9 sun u.h. 9in (22.5cm) u.s. 1ft (30cm)

Sarcoccoca humilis

An underestimated low evergreen shrub, sarcoccoca has small, dark green, shiny pointed leaves arranged alternately on branches up to 15in (37.5cm) high or sometimes a little more. The tiny flowers are creamy-white and start to bloom in late winter, spreading their sweet scent in the cold air. The flowers are followed by black berries. The plant spreads steadily by underground stolons and thrives under trees or in the shade of a wall, providing that the soil is fertile and well drained. Cuttings enhance indoor arrangements.

z 5-9 shade u.h. 15in (37.5cm)
u.s. 15in (37.5cm)

121

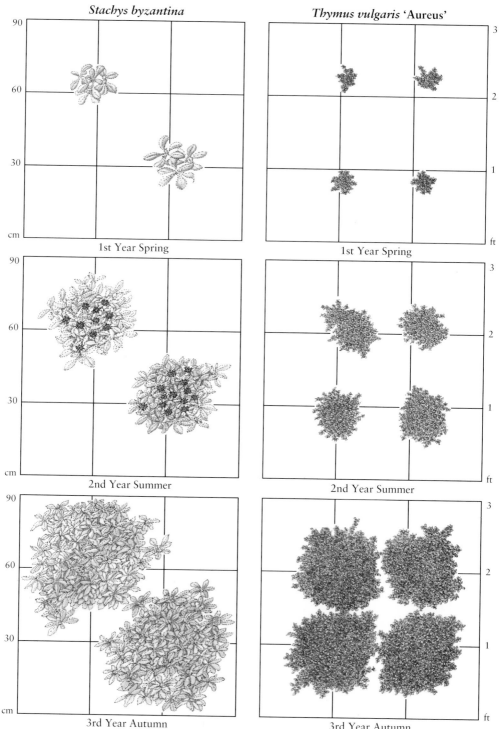

Stachys byzantina

Thymus vulgaris 'Aureus'

1st Year Spring

1st Year Spring

2nd Year Summer

2nd Year Summer

3rd Year Autumn

3rd Year Autumn

Vinca minor

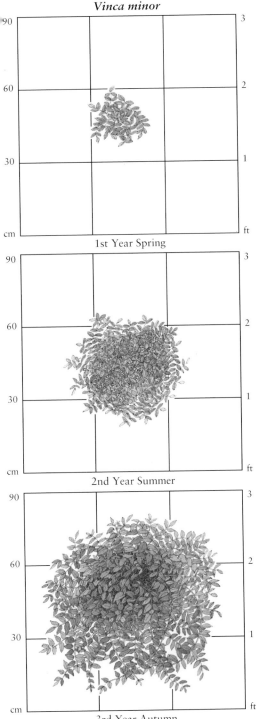

1st Year Spring

2nd Year Summer

3rd Year Autumn

Stachys byzantina

Bunnies' or lambs' ears
This plant is also called *S. lanata* and sometimes lambs' tongue. It has delightful soft, furry gray-white oval leaves, 1 to 4in (2.5-10cm) long, spreading carpet-like and smothering weeds all around. The flowers, which some people like to cut off, grow to 20in (50cm) tall in tight gray-purple whorls. The cultivar **'Silver Carpet'** does not produce flowers and is most suited to ground cover. Although evergreen the leaves get to be a bit ragged in winter, particularly in cold, damp conditions.

z 7-10 sun u.h. 4in (10cm) u.s. 18in (45cm)

Thymus vulgaris 'Aureus'

The culinary thyme, if grown in full sun and well-drained soil, is a hardy plant with dense, dark green foliage composed of small aromatic leaves. The cultivar 'Aureus' has tiny yellow-green leaves that need regular shearing to keep their intense color. **'Variegatus'** has gray-green leaves with narrow white edging. These two forms are sometimes classified under the species *T. citriodorus*. The pale purple flowers are arranged in small spikes, held on stalks a few inches above the leaves. To keep the plants bushy and compact cut back in the spring.

z 3-9 sun u.h. 8in (20cm) u.s. 1ft (30cm)

Vinca minor

Lesser periwinkle
This evergreen trailing perennial has shiny, oval, dark leaves about 1 to 2in (2.5-5cm) long. The bright bluey-mauve, star-shaped flowers appear in early to mid-spring and if the stems are cut back after flowering a second flush will come in late summer. In a well-drained, sunny position it can be invasive and needs severe curtailing. It tolerates shade and is also suitable for steep banks. **'Alba'** is white and **'Multiplex'** (double) is plum-purple. Some have variegated leaves.

z 4-9 sun or shade u.h. 8in (20cm)
u.s. 2ft (60cm)

Right: *Dictamnus albus purpureus* is an early summer-flowering perennial that should not be disturbed. The spikes of scented flowers stand 3ft (90cm) tall and the clumps spread up to 2ft (60cm). Violets and peonies are useful for the front of a border, where they will flower throughout the season.

Herbaceous perennials

Left: Hostas are mostly grown for their distinctive foliage. They make bold clumps of heart-shaped leaves in colors ranging from blue-green to palest yellow-cream, with cream and golden variegations. In summer most hostas display delicate purple or white flowers. The plant's chief enemies are slugs that can be deterred by surrounding the clumps with gravel or broken egg shells.

By definition, herbaceous perennials die down completely at the end of the growing season and overwinter underground until spring, when they grow up again in all their glory. They are endlessly rewarding: the sight of fresh strong growth emerging from the crowns in spring is appealing in itself, and the rest of the season is a long succession of blooms until the arrival of the first frosts.

The height of the summer is the climax of the year for herbaceous perennials. This is the time when cranesbills, poppies, delphiniums, lupines, penstemons, phlox and Shasta daisies are at their best. The foliage of plants that have finished or have yet to bloom can provide an attractive backdrop to these summer perennials, in all their glory.

Herbaceous perennials vary in height from 7ft (2.1m) down to 6in (15cm), giving great scope for planting from the

back to the front of a border. This range also allows perennials to be combined with shrubs and bulbs, tall species complementing shrubs, small plants covering dying bulb foliage.

Tall, floppy perennials need to be supported, particularly in exposed, windy or shady gardens. There are many different types of metallic or plastic-coated stakes and hoops available; these should be positioned early, before the plants actually need them. They are effective but somewhat ugly, and more natural looking pea-sticks may be preferred. Do not have too many plants that need supporting in the same area: an array of stakes is not very pleasing.

It is not always easy to get the design of a border right at the first attempt and the opportunity after one, two or three years to lift, split and re-site plants is very useful. Surplus plants can be given away to fellow gardeners. If this is not possible, do not be afraid of discarding unwanted plants onto the compost heap – your garden will benefit both from the thinning out and from the vegetable matter.

Some species spread faster than expected, swamping neighbors, and a vigilant eye is needed. It is, however, surprising how well some plants survive being covered by other perennials. This is a quality to exploit in a design, using later-flowering species to fill a void left by those that have finished. For example, billowy clouds of gypsophila, planted behind a clump of *Incarvillea delavayi*, will completely hide the latter's fading flowers and dying leaves during the second half of the summer, without harming the plant beneath.

Most species are clump-forming, spreading by creeping rhizomes, while others seed themselves with abandon. In certain conditions, some plants can be invasive. *Lythrum salicaria*, *Saponaria officinalis* and *Macleaya microphylla* are particular culprits in many soils, and the smallest piece of root will spread like wildfire (although in some soils these plants are difficult to establish). Seedlings of lady's mantle and fennel need pulling up relentlessly to keep them in check. In most cases it is necessary to lift and split clumps regularly or the plants become congested and cease to flower profusely. There are exceptions: for example, most peonies do not like to be disturbed.

A perennial border will usefully provide quantities of cut flowers for indoor arrangements, as most species benefit from regular cutting, which promotes new growth and a longer flowering period. Thorough dead-heading has the same effect for many plants and it also prevents an excessive number of random seedlings from germinating. Some plants, such as many of the alliums and *Sedum spectabile*, have beautiful seed heads that can be used in dried floral arrangements. Alternatively, these can be left on the plant, to form dramatic silhouettes in winter frosts.

Herbaceous perennials should be

Left: A traditional British herbaceous border at the height of the summer. Such a large area requires hours of regular attention to maintain it at its peak, but a smaller border can be kept under control with minimal effort. The most important task is to lift and split the most vigorous plants, to prevent them from swamping smaller ones. Do this during the autumn or spring.

Below: An attractive pairing of *Penstemon* 'Garnet' and *Sidalcea* 'Rose Queen'. The flowering seasons of these plants can be significantly extended by dead-heading.

planted no deeper than they were in the nursery bed or container and they should be thoroughly firmed, making sure that no air pockets are left. Shallow-rooted species have a tendency to become dislodged in the first cold of winter: as the soil freezes and thaws alternately the ground heaves and exposes the roots.

Perhaps the single most important cultivation technique available to the gardener when growing herbaceous perennials is mulching. This helps to conserve soil moisture and protects the roots from extremes of temperature, as well as discouraging weeds from germinating. Mulches can be of well-rotted mushroom compost or leaf mold, gravel, shredded forest bark or coconut fiber, and should be 2 to 3in (5-7.5cm) deep. Over the years, organic mulches gradually break down and are worked into the soil by worms. The best time to apply mulch is just after planting or in spring when the borders are being tidied. The bed should be weed-free and well watered before spreading the mulch, which must not settle too close to the crown of the plants as this tends to encourage pests and disease. Finally, a satisfying bonus is that mulches give a border a well-cultivated and cared for appearance.

In cold climates, some winter protection may be necessary, particularly for young plants and marginally hardy species. The best materials for this are

Right: In a moist shady position the foliage of *Rheum palmatum*, *Pulmonaria saccharata* and *Iris pseudacorus* cover the ground long after the plants have finished flowering. But by winter these banks will be bare of vegetation.
Below: An effective gradation of sizes and colors in a sunny position: clumps of *Alchemilla mollis* and the creeping *Alstroemeria* are backed by the shrubby mallow, *Lavatera olbia*.

salt hay, clean straw, pine needles or branches of evergreens, loosely laid over the crowns of the plants and anchored down with soil, gravel or stones. These dry rapidly after rain, which is an essential quality as exposure to constant damp will rot and kill the crown. Fallen leaves are not suitable as they retain moisture (as will straw if the atmosphere is constantly damp). The aim is to maintain the soil at an even temperature throughout the winter; it is advisable to spread the mulch just after the soil has dropped in temperature or has just frozen. The later the mulch is applied, the less likely it will become the winter home of mice and voles.

An additional safeguard, well-worth the effort, is to take cuttings in late summer of any treasured plant that may not survive the winter.

THE GROWTH CHARTS

Plants are illustrated in the growth charts in groups of three as perennials are rarely grown in isolation; species have been selected on the basis of complementary colors, heights and periods of interest. Plants that grow up to about 3ft (90cm) are featured on p. 130-151; those that reach 6ft (180cm) are shown on p. 152-161.

The spread of clumps of each species is shown beside the corresponding entry. Three years' growth is shown using different shades of green: the lightest shade represents the first year's growth, the darkest the third.

Polygonum bistorta 'Superbum'   *Paeonia officinalis*   *Polygonatum × hybridum*

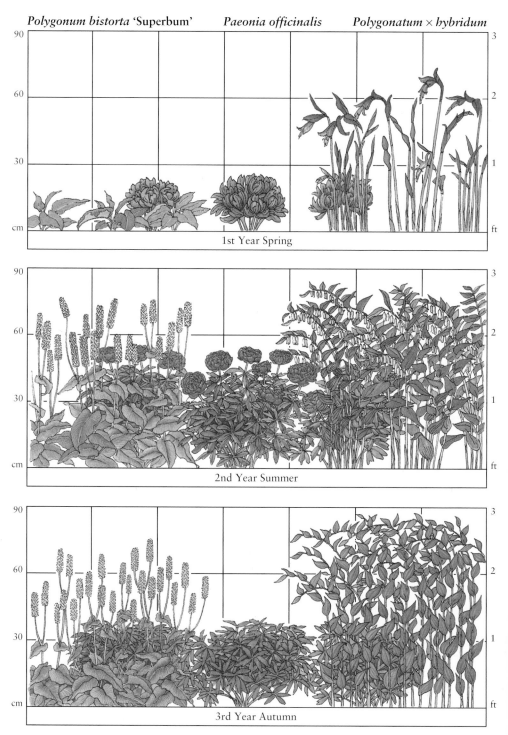

1st Year Spring

2nd Year Summer

3rd Year Autumn

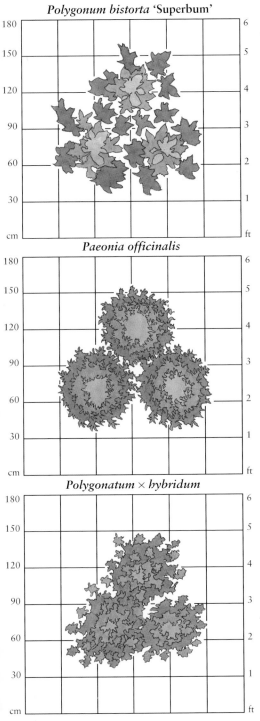

Polygonum bistorta 'Superbum'

This superb bistort makes strong clumps of wide, pointed, mid-green basal leaves, up to 10in (25cm) long, with a soft, leathery texture. Slender stems rise to 2½ft (75cm), topped with narrow bottlebrush spikes of pale pink flowers from early to late summer, lasting longest in moist conditions. The plant spreads by underground rhizomes. The species is smaller and is sometimes called snakeroot or snakesweed. *Polygonum amplexicaule* '**Atrosanguineum**' is bolder with rich crimson flower spikes from early summer through to the first frosts.

z 3-9 sun or partial shade

Paeonia officinalis

European herbaceous peony

This plant does not like being moved but it will survive for years against all competition and impossible odds. It can make 3ft (90cm) wide clumps of deeply divided mid-green foliage that lasts throughout the growing season. The flowers are deep velvety red, 3 to 5in (7.5-12.5cm) wide, and are most commonly found in the full double form, '**Rubra Plena**'. *P.* '**Festiva Maxima**' and '**Sarah Bernhardt**' are also double; *P.* '**Bowl of Beauty**', '**Gold Standard**' and '**Pink Tranquility**' are single.

z 2-10 sun or partial shade

Polygonatum × hybridum

Solomon's seal

This plant quickly forms arching stems up to 3ft (90cm) tall with translucent opposite leaves, 2 to 6in (5-15cm) long, that are oval and pointed at the end. The small cream bell-shaped flowers, edged in green, hide under the leaves in late spring and early summer. '**Variegatum**', with creamy striped leaves, is less vigorous. *P. canaliculatum* (alternatively listed as *P. commutatum* or *P. biflorum*) is a giant form growing to 6ft (1.8m) with 4 to 8in (10-20cm) leaves, clusters of bell-shaped flowers, and often black berries.

z 4-9 shade

131

Rudbeckia fulgida 'Goldsturm'   Euphorbia polychroma   Doronicum 'Miss Mason'

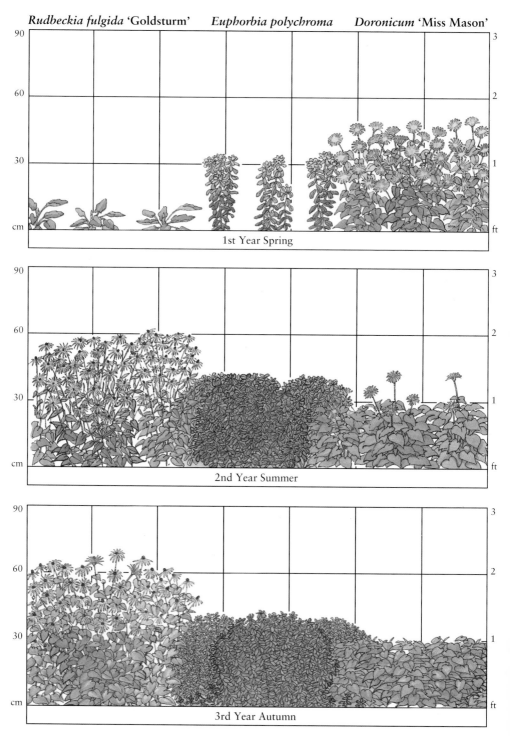

1st Year Spring

2nd Year Summer

3rd Year Autumn

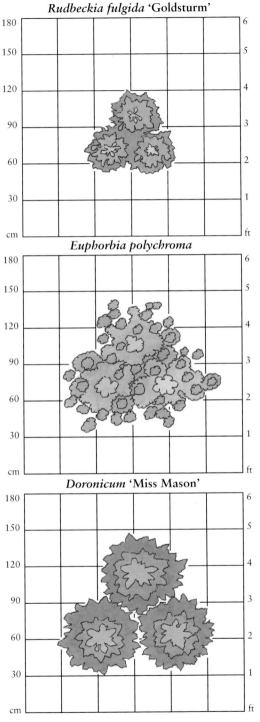

Rudbeckia fulgida 'Goldsturm'

The black-eyed susan is a native of the north American prairie. It is easy to grow for the late summer and, en masse, presents a host of flowers. 'Goldsturm' is one of the best selections with 3 to 4in (7.5-10cm) bright daisy flowers that have warm yellow thin rays that point downwards and velvety black centers in the shape of a cone. The flower stems are up to 2ft (60cm) tall with numerous narrow oval basal leaves some 6in (15cm) or more long. It spreads quickly by rhizomes in any fertile, reasonably moisture-retentive soil and is long lived.

z 3-9 sun or partial shade

Euphorbia polychroma

This is a striking species that emerges early in spring, resembling a cushion, and quickly grows to 18in (45cm) tall. Sulphur-yellow flower heads are held above fresh green leaves which spread to 18in (45cm). The flowers fade in summer to green, turning reddy-brown in autumn. *E. characias wulfenii* is a much larger species, nearly 3ft (90cm) high and wide. It is not so hardy (z 7) and has glaucous foilage and yellow-green flowers which appear on two-year-old stems.
E. griffithii grows and spreads to 2ft (60cm) and has deep orange flower heads.

z 4-10 sun or partial shade

Doronicum 'Miss Mason'

This perennial grows happily in most soils, developing from tough rhizomes that steadily multiply to make a clump about 2ft (60cm) wide. Probably a cross between the leopard's bane varieties *D. orientale* and *D. austriacum*, it is a superb plant that flowers after daffodils and at the same time as the perennial honesty and early euphorbias. The leaves are heart-shaped, up to 3in (7.5cm) long, with toothed edges. The bright yellow daisy flowers are up to 3in (7.5cm) wide on 18in (45cm) stems. It does best in well-drained, moisture-rententive soil.

z 4-9 sun or partial shade

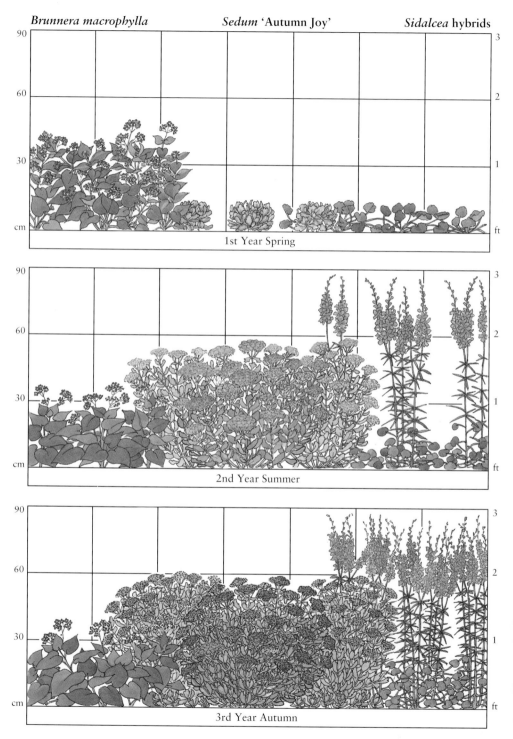

1st Year Spring

2nd Year Summer

3rd Year Autumn

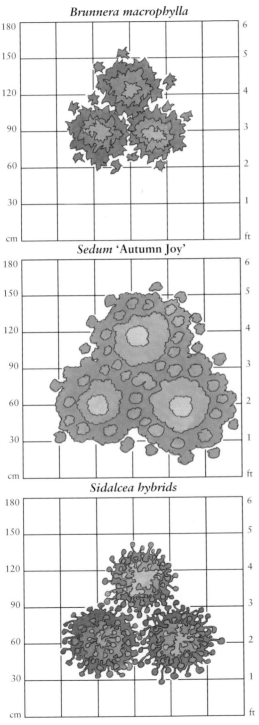

Brunnera macrophylla

This spring-flowering perennial is reminiscent of forget-me-nots and hails from Russia. A good ground cover plant, it makes substantial rounded clumps of large mid-green, heart-shaped leaves 3 to 6in (7.5-15cm) long. The small sprays of vivid blue flowers hover above the leaves on stems 1ft (30cm) or more tall. The plant will spread to 2ft (60cm) or so and should be split every three or four years. The variegated form, 'Dawson's White', has bold creamy-white mottling on the leaves and is slightly less vigorous. Brunneras prefer a moist soil.

z 3-9 shade

Sedum 'Autumn Joy'

This remarkable plant is attractive all through the year. The young growth of fleshy gray-green crinkly-edged leaves appears in spring, followed in summer by large flat flower heads in the same color on 2ft (60cm) stems. The flowers turn pink through the summer (when they attract myriads of butterflies) and finally, in autumn, copper-red. The dried seed heads subsist well into the winter and when cut down in late winter the following year's growth is already emerging. In fertile soil the plant quickly makes a bold clump 2ft (60cm) wide.

z 4-9 sun or partial shade

Sidalcea hybrids

Sidalceas resemble small hollyhocks. They make well-rounded clumps up to 18in (45cm) wide. The weed-smothering, long-stalked basal leaves are some 3in (7.5cm) wide with up to nine lobes and crenellated edges. The flower stems, 3 to 4ft (90-120cm) tall, have smaller, more deeply lobed leaves and terminate with imposing branched spikes of pink cupped flowers, 2in (5cm) wide, with characteristically notched petals. These vary in color from deep red in 'Croftway Red' to pale pink in 'Elsie Heugh'. Grow in moisture-retentive, well-drained soil.

z 5-9 sun or partial shade

Aconitum 'Bressingham Spire'   Astilbe × arendsii   Anemone 'Honorine Jobert'

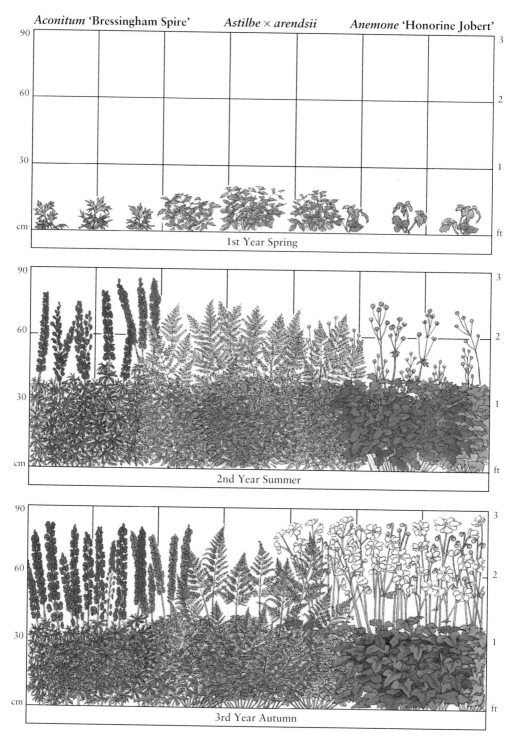

1st Year Spring

2nd Year Summer

3rd Year Autumn

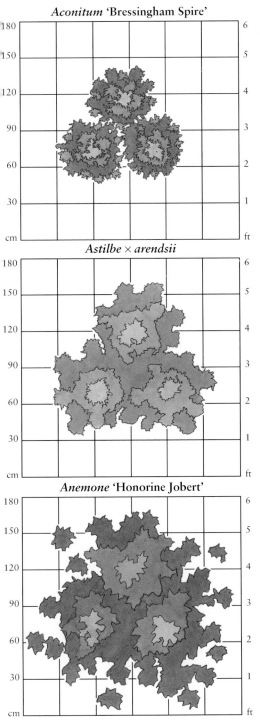

Aconitum 'Bressingham Spire'

Aconitum 'Bressingham Spire'

A cultivar of monkshood, this is a valuable hardy perennial that flowers in late summer and early autumn. It stands 3ft (90cm) high, with erect panicles of helmet-shaped deep purple-blue flowers. The foliage is deeply lobed. Easy to grow in rich, cool, moisture-retentive soil, improved by a mulch in the spring, it spreads to 18in (45cm). The tuberous roots (which are poisonous) need dividing every three to four years to encourage strong stem growth. Do this in late autumn or early winter as the plants start into growth in late winter or early spring.

z 3-8 sun or partial shade.

Astilbe × arendsii

Astilbe × arendsii

These fine perennials have delicate foliage and feathery flowers that last throughout the summer. The leaves are deeply cut, in dark shades of bronzy-green that set off the flower plumes spectacularly. The range of colors is huge, from white (**'Bridal Veil'**) through tints of rose pink (**'Venus'**) and pink and salmon (**'Federsee'**) to dark crimson (**'Fanal'**). Flower height varies from 1½ to 2½ft (45-75cm) and plants spread to about 2½ft (75cm). Astilbes require a deep soil rich in organic matter that retains plenty of moisture throughout the growing season.

z 4-8 partial shade

Anemone 'Honorine Jobert'

Anemone 'Honorine Jobert'

The beautiful Japanese anemones flower for up to three months from mid-summer to autumn. The common form has pink saucer-shaped flowers with a cluster of yellow stamens. 'Honorine Jobert' has clear white petals, highlighted by the yellow stamens. Although the branching flower stems stand up to 3ft (90cm) high they require no staking. The leaves are deeply lobed, up to 4in (10cm) wide and form a neat mound under the flower stems. In a good heavy soil these anemones spread 2ft (60cm) but in a light soil they are rampant.

z 5-8 sun or partial shade

Dicentra spectabilis   *Hosta sieboldiana* 'Elegans'   *Monarda didyma* 'Cambridge Scarlet'

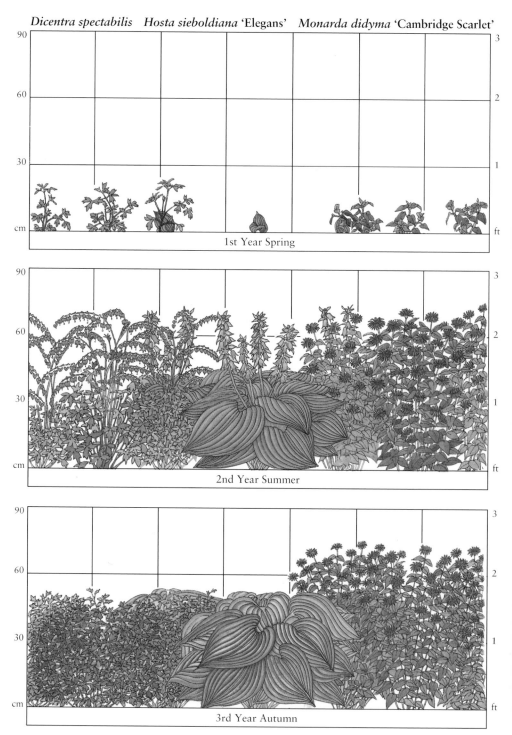

1st Year Spring

2nd Year Summer

3rd Year Autumn

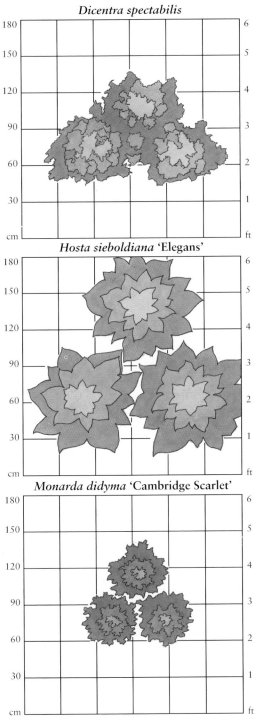

Dicentra spectabilis

Bleeding heart, lady's locket or Dutchman's breeches
The delicate, glaucous green, fern-like foliage of this plant is among the first to appear in spring. The graceful arching stems are up to 2ft (60cm) tall and are hung with beautiful deep bluey-pink heart-shaped flowers that have white tips. There is a pure white form, *alba*, with a good variety named **'Pantaloons'**. *D. eximia* and *D. formosa* are two smaller species that are also useful ground cover in cool conditions. *D. spectabilis* becomes dormant at mid-summer in hot conditions.

z 3-9 sun or partial shade

Hosta sieboldiana 'Elegans'

Plantain lilies are among the most rewarding of ground-covering herbaceous perennials. The many species and cultivars have lanceolate or broad leaves, ranging from deep blue-green to palest yellow, or they have gold and silver variegations. The purple, mauve or white flowers are small, although some are scented. Slugs and snails are a menace and will be hindered by a ring of gravel; or the plants can be grown in tall pots. *H. sieboldiana* 'Elegans' makes sizeable clumps of large rounded glaucous leaves. Hostas need moisture-retentive soil.

z 3-10 sun or shade

Monarda didyma 'Cambridge Scarlet'

Bee balm, bergamot or oswego tea
Aromatic oval leaves, 2 to 4in (5-10cm) long, are sharply pointed at the tips. Strange hooded flowers, particularly attractive to bees and hummingbirds, are borne in circular heads at the top of stiff erect square stems up to 18in (45cm) tall. The summer flowering season can be extended by dead-heading. The spreading clumps need dividing every three or four years. Other good cultivars include **'Croftway Pink'**, salmon pink, **'Snow White'**, white, **'Mahogany'**, brownish-red, and **'Adam'**, cerise-red (more compact).

z 4-9 sun or partial shade

Scabiosa caucasica   *Geranium endressii* 'A. T. Johnson'   *Catananche caerulea* 'Major'

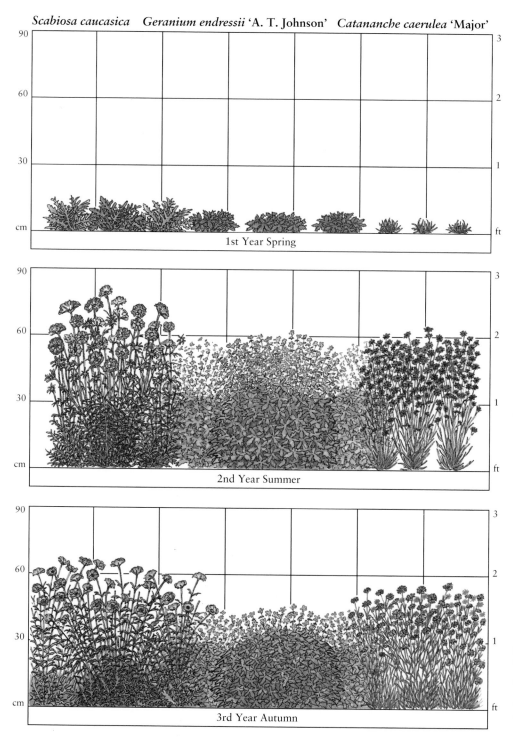

1st Year Spring

2nd Year Summer

3rd Year Autumn

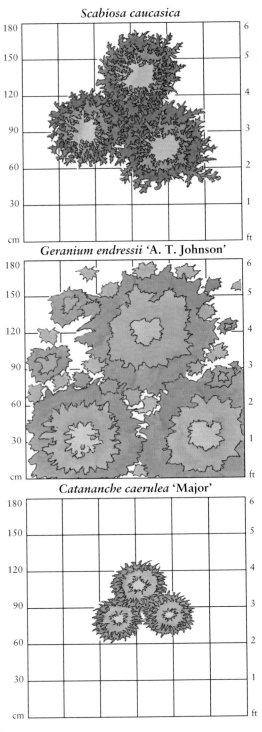

Scabiosa caucasica

Geranium endressii 'A. T. Johnson'

Catananche caerulea 'Major'

Scabiosa caucasica

This beautiful perennial scabious is a native of the limestone Caucasus Mountains and will be short lived if grown in acid soil. A little lime will improve flowering performance in acid conditions. The leaves are narrow at the base and divided further up the 2 to 2½ft (60-75cm) stems. The lavender-blue pincushion flowers are about 2in (5cm) wide and bloom from early to late summer. There are some good color forms such as 'Clive Greaves', violet-blue, 'Miss Willmott', creamy white, and 'Bressingham White', pure white.

z 3-9 sun

Geranium endressii 'A.T. Johnson'

This pretty ground-covering plant is not too vigorous, spreading to about 3ft (90cm), and will not choke other plants. The foliage makes neat clumps of deeply divided long-stalked leaves 2 to 3in (5-7.5cm) wide. The plentiful light pink flowers are about 1in (2.5cm) wide on stems up to 2ft (60cm) long and blossom throughout summer. 'Wargrave Pink' has bright salmon pink flowers. *Geranium* 'Johnson's Blue' is one of the best blue forms; *G. macrorrhizum* has slightly aromatic leaves, pale green at first, russet in autumn, and soft pink flowers.

z 3-8 sun or partial shade

Catananche caerulea 'Major'

The perennial cupid's dart or blue cupidone was once used in love potions: the genus name comes from the Greek word for "strong incentive". Beautiful crisp blue flowers in a papery calyx blossom from early summer to early autumn on 2ft (60cm) wiry stems. The grassy foliage is gray-green and makes crowns up to 1ft (30cm) wide that can be divided every year or two to extend the life of the plant. Root cuttings can be taken. Other good cultivars are 'Perry's White' and 'Bicolor'. They like well-drained soil and withstand drought.

z 4-9 sun

141

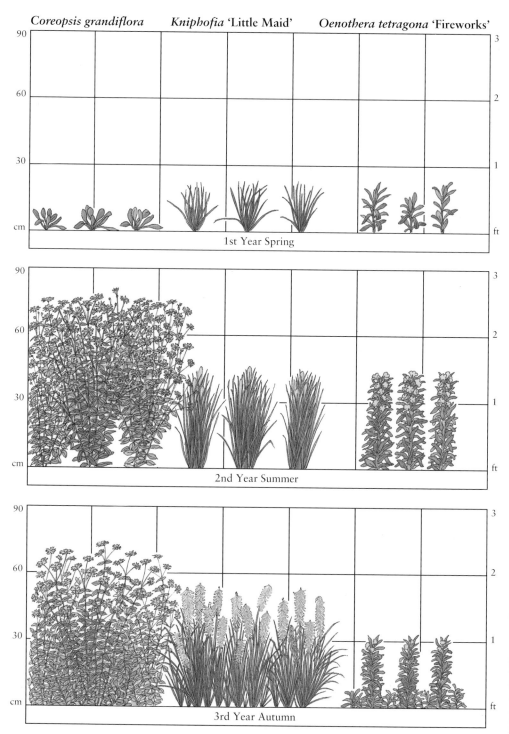

Coreopsis grandiflora   *Kniphofia* 'Little Maid'   *Oenothera tetragona* 'Fireworks'

1st Year Spring

2nd Year Summer

3rd Year Autumn

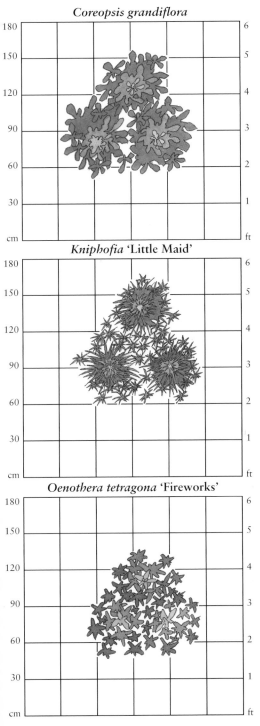

Coreopsis grandiflora

Coreopsis grandiflora

The bright yellow flowers of this perennial provide a splash of sunshine in the border throughout the summer and into early autumn. The narrow leaves are occasionally lobed. Stems of 1½ to 2ft (45-60cm) long or more carry flowers some 2in (5cm) wide; the ray florets are split at the tip and have a small dark maroon spot at the base. The "daisy" disk is yellow and relatively small. Among the best cultivars are **'Goldfink'**, **'Mayfield Giant'**, **'Badengold'** and **'Sunburst'**. All need moist but well-drained soil.

z 3-10 sun

Kniphofia 'Little Maid'

Kniphofia **'Little Maid'**

The most frequently seen red hot poker is gaudy, with nearly 3ft (90cm) tall erect stems and pale yellow and scarlet stiff inflorescences. There are many more tasteful species and cultivars which deserve a place in the border. 'Little Maid' is one of the daintiest, with grassy bluey-green foliage and short stems 2ft (60cm) tall; the flower spikes are pale lemon-yellow, fading to cream from the base up as they age. Other flowers range from deep red to apricot orange and bright yellow. Sharply draining soil is recommended, as is winter protection.

z 5-9 sun

Oenothera tetragona 'Fireworks'

Oenothera tetragona

The broad, oval leaves of this evening primrose are 1 to 3in (2.5-7.5cm) long, have wavy edges and are dark green above and bluish beneath. But it is the bright yellow cupped summer flowers, 1 to 2in (2.5-5cm) wide, that are this plant's chief attraction. These are borne on 1 to 2ft (30-60cm) stems, are reddish in bud and open in the late afternoon. One of the best forms of this variable species is **'Fireworks'** ('Fyrverkeri') which has deep red buds and rosettes of rich purple-green young foliage. It does best in well-drained soil.

z 4-9 sun

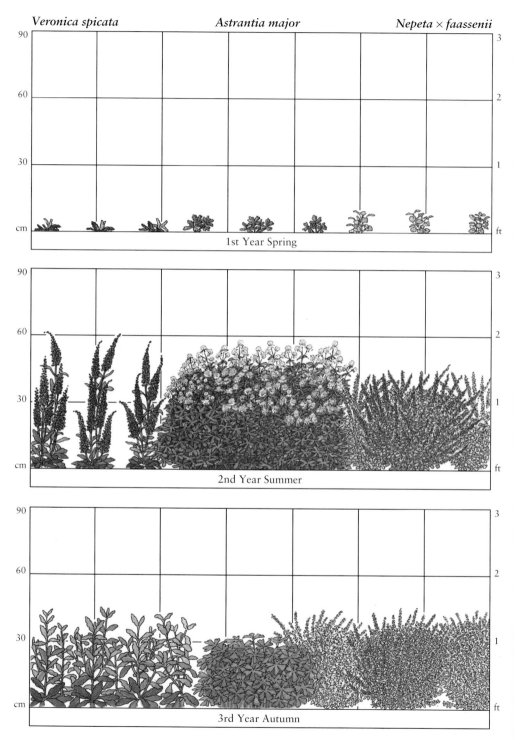

Veronica spicata   *Astrantia major*   *Nepeta × faassenii*

1st Year Spring

2nd Year Summer

3rd Year Autumn

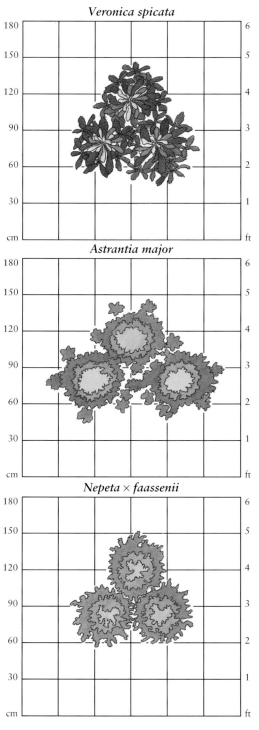

Veronica spicata

Veronica spicata

Selections of the variable wild form of the spiked speedwell make neat, compact garden plants. The 3in (7.5cm) leaves are narrowly oval with crenate edges. The small deep blue flowers are borne in terminal spikes on erect stems up to 1 or 2ft (30-60cm) tall. Veronicas have been extensively hybridized and cultivars include 'Icicle' (white), 'Crater Lake Blue' (dark blue), 'Barcarolle' (pink), and 'Red Fox' (reddish-pink). They grow best in well-drained, fertile soil and are tolerant of dry conditions, spreading to 18in (45cm).

z 4-9 sun or partial shade

Astrantia major

Astrantia major

The basal foliage of this perennial is deeply divided and makes good ground cover from which the branched flower stems emerge. Each blossom resembles a little red pincushion stuck with green and white florets and is surrounded by a frill of bracts; en masse they create a charming billowy effect. 'Rubra' has plum-colored flowers; 'Shaggy' has larger, dissected leaves and frillier collars; 'Sunningdale Variegated' has creamy-white splashes on the leaves. Astrantias, commonly called masterwort, like plenty of moisture and spread by underground runners.

z 4-8 sun or partial shade

Nepeta × faassenii

Nepeta × faassenii
Catmint

An aromatic plant that is a favorite with cats who will roll in a clump until the foliage almost disappears. It has gray-green soft downy foliage that is scented and tumbles over. The 18in (45cm) stems are covered with purple-blue flower spikes in late spring and early summer, and again in autumn if the plant is sheared back after flowering. There is a compact selection, 'Blue Wonder', that only reaches 15in (37.5cm) and a hybrid version, 'Six Hills Giant', which reaches 3ft (90cm). It thrives in the poorest soils.

z 3-9 sun

145

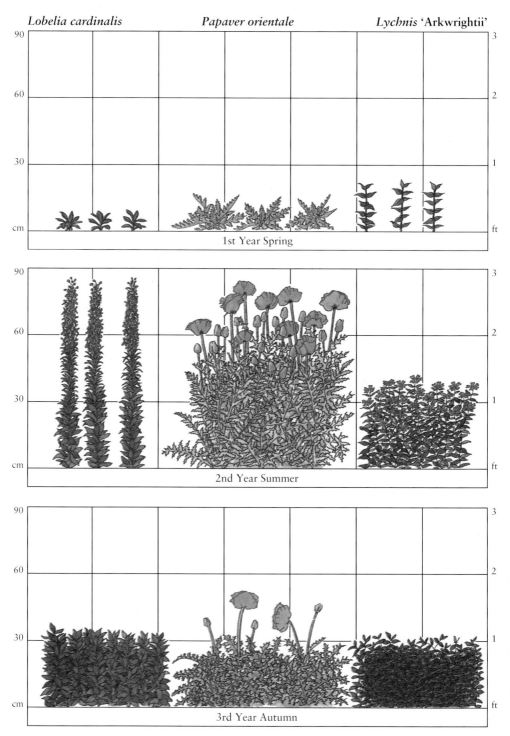

Lobelia cardinalis   Papaver orientale   Lychnis 'Arkwrightii'

1st Year Spring

2nd Year Summer

3rd Year Autumn

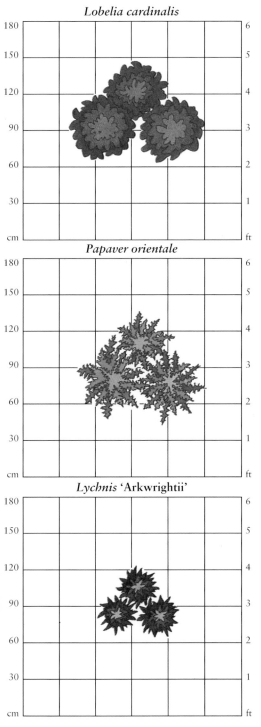

Lobelia cardinalis

Lobelia cardinalis

Cardinal flower

The herbaceous lobelias require heavy, moisture-laden soils to succeed. They are tall, elegant plants that flower from mid-summer to early autumn and range from scarlet to deep-blue with some white forms. *L. cardinalis* has striking rosettes, up to 8in (20cm) wide, of claret-red oval leaves, 3 to 4in (7.5-10cm) long. These form spikes on stems of a similar color, 2 to 3ft (60-90cm) tall. **L. syphilitica** bears blue flowers on 3ft (90cm) stems for up to six weeks in the summer. It seeds itself with abandon.

z 2-8 partial shade

Papaver orientale

Papaver orientale

Oriental poppy

This is one of the most opulent sights of early summer. The hairy basal leaves some 10in (25cm) long have dissected edges and form sprawling 2ft (60cm) clumps. The flowers have papery petals and can be up to 4 or 5in (10-12.5cm) wide. These are held on gently curving stems up to 3ft (90cm) long and vary in color from scarlet to white. Cultivars include '**Harvest Moon**', golden orange, '**Raspberry Queen**', pink, and '**Perry's White**', gray-white with a maroon basal blotch. Poppies do best in dry soils.

z 3-9 sun

Lychnis 'Arkwrightii'

Lychnis 'Arkwrightii'

The color of this hybrid maltese cross has an electric quality that makes it stand out in any border. It forms clumps up to 1ft (30cm) wide and grows to 18in (45cm) tall. The slightly feeble stems are clothed in dark green oval leaves and carry brilliant orange-red five-petaled flowers. *L. coronaria* has great clumps of gray furry leaves and bright purple-cerise flowers; the more unusual white form, *alba*, comes true from seed but if you grow both together they tend to hybridize and fewer whites are produced. These plants need well-drained soil.

z 4-9 sun

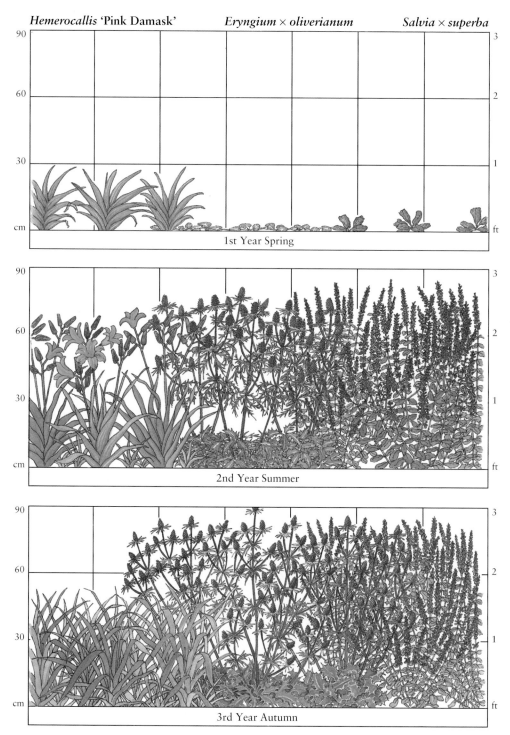

Hemerocallis 'Pink Damask'   *Eryngium* × *oliverianum*   *Salvia* × *superba*

1st Year Spring

2nd Year Summer

3rd Year Autumn

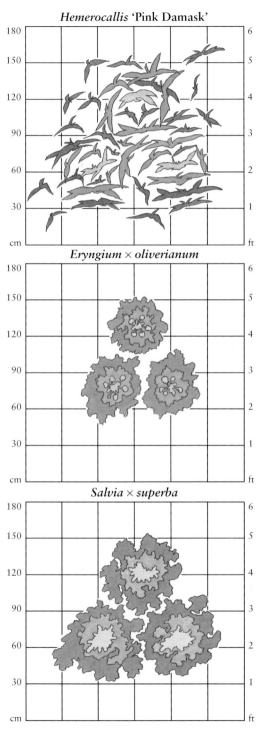

Hemerocallis 'Pink Damask'

Hemerocallis 'Pink Damask'

Daylilies are among the most robust of garden plants: surviving drought and copious amounts of water, they can be transplanted at any time of the year. Although each flower lasts for only a day the succession continues steadily for two or three weeks. The two oldest garden species in cultivation, *H. fulva* and *H. flava*, spread by rhizomes and can prove a weed, but many recent hybrids have compact root systems, and only require splitting when the clump ceases to flower freely. These range in color from maroon to palest yellow.

z 3-10 sun

Eryngium × oliverianum

This is one of the prickly metallic blue perennials that last so well in the summer. The genus is commonly called sea hollies, although the sea holly is specifically *E. maritimum*. *E. × oliverianum* forms rosettes of persistent basal leaves, rounded and toothed, from 3 to 6in (7.5-15cm) long, with cream veins. The flower stems are just over 2ft (60cm) tall and bear blue-green, spiny palmate leaves. The flowers look like small spiky thimbles in prickly bracts. The biennial Miss Willmott's ghost, *E. giganteum*, is 3ft (90cm) tall. They like well-drained soil.

z 5-10 sun

Salvia × superba

Related to the culinary sage, this decorative plant can reach 3ft (90cm) or more. It has stiff square stems and oval dull green toothed leaves. Spikes of ½in (1cm) flowers form in summer, opening deep violet-purple and surrounded by crimson bracts which are most prominent early in the season. A second flush in early autumn can be encouraged by cutting the plants right back as the first blossoms fade; this also prevents the plant from getting too leggy. **'East Friesland'** and **'May Night'** are the hardiest cultivars. Good drainage is essential.

z 5-9 sun

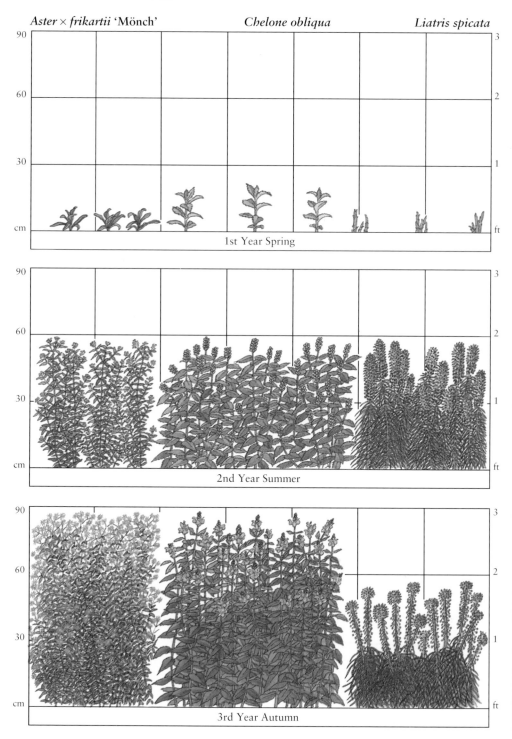

Aster × frikartii 'Mönch' *Chelone obliqua* *Liatris spicata*

1st Year Spring

2nd Year Summer

3rd Year Autumn

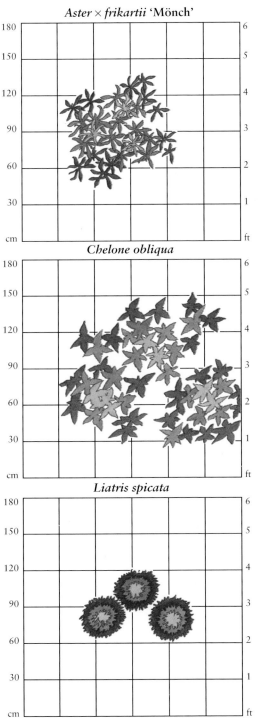

Aster × *frikartii* 'Mönch'

This is one of the best autumn-flowering perennials and lasts from late summer to mid- or late autumn. It has large scented bluey-mauve daisy flowers with yellow centers that can be encouraged to bloom more freely by pinching back the stems in spring and early summer. The upright stems are nearly 3ft (90cm) tall and do not need staking. It is easy to grow in any well-drained soil, spreading to 15in (37.5cm), and should be divided every three or four years. The cultivar **'Wonder of Staffa'** is similar in color but shorter at up to 2ft (60cm) and hardier (z 4).

z 6-9 sun or partial shade

Chelone obliqua

Rose turtle's head or shell-flower
This intriguing plant is useful in the late summer border. Its strangely shaped, weather-resistant deep lilac flowers earn it its common names. The leaves are dark green and clearly veined. They are abundant at the base and continue in opposite pairs all the way up the 3ft (90cm) stems. There are two rarer forms worth looking out for: the white variety *alba* and a dwarf clone, **'Praecox Nana'**, that flowers in late summer. All forms require moist but not waterlogged conditions.

z 4-9 partial shade

Liatris spicata

An attractive gayfeather for a well-drained site, this plant makes clumps of dark green grassy foliage. The leafy stems are topped with bottlebrush flowers that are unusual in that they open from the top down. The most common selection is the rosy-mauve **'Kobold'** which is up to 18in (45cm) tall. White flowers are found on **'Alba'** and the taller *L. scariosa* **'Alba Magnifica'** which reaches 3ft (90cm) and has lighter green foliage. They are easy to grow, only requiring dead-heading after flowering in summer and rarely needing dividing.

z 3-10 sun

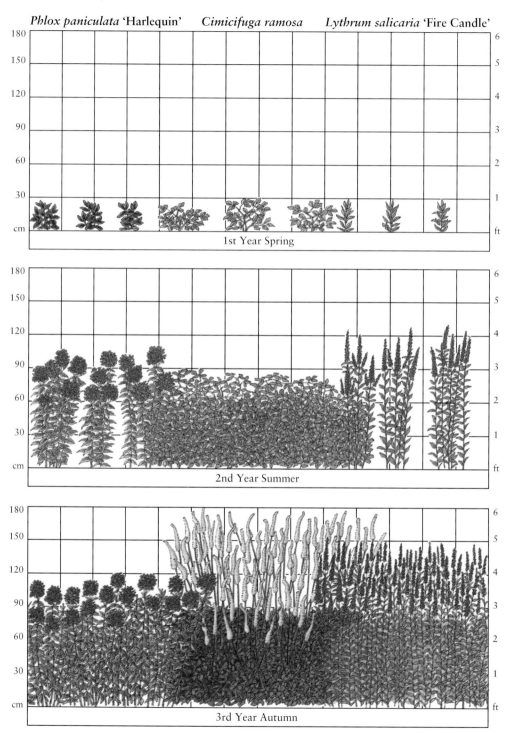

Phlox paniculata 'Harlequin'   *Cimicifuga ramosa*   *Lythrum salicaria* 'Fire Candle'

1st Year Spring

2nd Year Summer

3rd Year Autumn

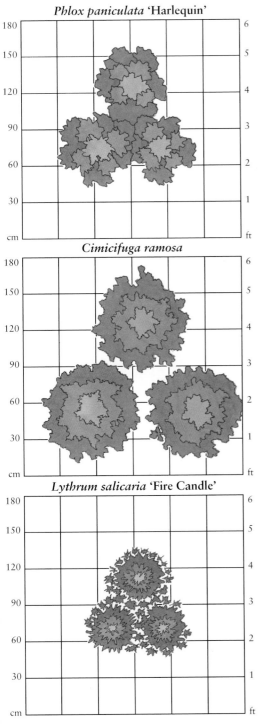

Phlox paniculata 'Harlequin'

Cimicifuga ramosa

Lythrum salicaria 'Fire Candle'

Phlox paniculata hybrids

The rewards of phlox are worth every minute spent providing them with a deep humus-rich and freely draining soil and plenty of nutrients and water in the growing season. They have extravagantly colorful blooms in shades of white, orange, pink, purple, lilac and lavender. These last a long time during the summer. Strong growth will be ensured by pinching back any weak shoots. A new if lighter crop of blooms will appear in the early autumn if the first ones are cut back as soon as they fade. Select mildew-resistant cultivars.

z 3-9 sun or partial shade

Cimicifuga ramosa

This superb bugbane tolerates shade without leaning toward the light. Pure white bottlebrush inflorescences up to 1ft (30cm) long enliven the garden in late summer and early autumn. These are carried on slender, branched stems that can be 7ft (2.1m) long. Green seed pods remain on the plant well into winter and can be used in dry arrangements. The large divided leaves are attractive all summer, making a mound 4ft (1.2m) across that turns yellow in the late autumn. '**Atropurpurea**' has purple foliage. They like a cool moist soil.

z 3-9 shade or partial sun

Lythrum salicaria 'Fire Candle'

This adaptable purple loosestrife requires ordinary soil and tolerates moist or dry conditions; in some situations it can be invasive. It has 3in (7.5cm) oval leaves, pointed at the end, that are arranged in pairs up the stems; these hold terminal spikes of deep rose red flowers. The total height is 3ft (90cm) and a plant will spread to 18in (45cm). It blossoms in mid-summer. The cultivar '**Morden's Pink**' has pinker flowers from early summer to early autumn, is particularly hardy and is more vigorous, growing to 4ft (1.2m) and spreading up to 3ft (90cm).

z 3-9 sun or partial shade

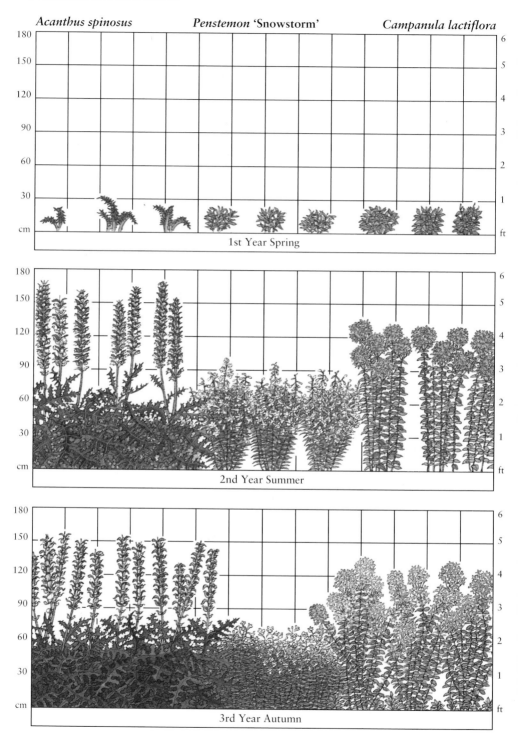

Acanthus spinosus   *Penstemon 'Snowstorm'*   *Campanula lactiflora*

1st Year Spring

2nd Year Summer

3rd Year Autumn

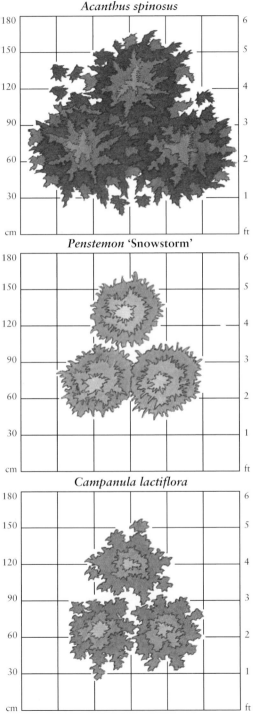

Acanthus spinosus

It is the architectural quality of this bear's breeches that makes it such an asset. The deeply cut dark shiny green leaves reach 2 to 3ft (60-90cm) in length and are midway between *A. mollis* and *A. spinosissimus* for spikiness. The stiff, prickly flower stems are at least 4ft (1.2m) tall and toward the end of summer are clothed nearly all the way up with hooded purple and white flowers. It can be invasive, spreading by rhizomes to 2 or 3ft (60-90cm). It likes sharply draining soil and can be used as a foliage plant in partial shade.

z 5-9 sun

Penstemon 'Snowstorm'

There are approximately 250 species and forms of penstemons available in the United States, ranging in color from deep red to white with varying shades of blue. They also range in hardiness; it is said that the wider the leaf the more tender the plant. *P. barbatus* and *P. ovatus* hybrids are the most cold-tolerant. Their greatest asset is the length of their flowering season, from early to late summer, which can be extended well into autumn by dead-heading. The tubular flowers of 'Snowstorm' are pure white. Penstemons need good drainage.

z 8-10 sun or partial shade

Campanula lactiflora

One of the most beautiful and easiest to grow campanulas. It has tall thick stems to 4ft (1.2m) that are clothed with pointed leaves. During the summer these are topped by large branching heads covered with pale lilac bell-flowers. 'Pritchard's Variety' is slightly shorter with stems to 3ft (90cm) and deep violet-blue flowers; 'Loddon Anna' has tall stems to 4 or 5ft (1.2-1.5m) and pale pink bells. It is possible to extend the flowering season of these three plants by cutting back some of the stems in late spring. All require moisture.

z 4-9 sun or partial shade

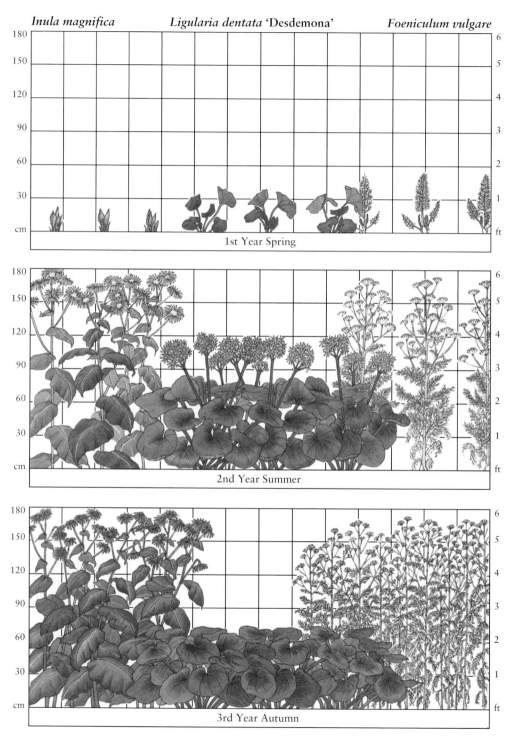

Inula magnifica   *Ligularia dentata* 'Desdemona'   *Foeniculum vulgare*

1st Year Spring

2nd Year Summer

3rd Year Autumn

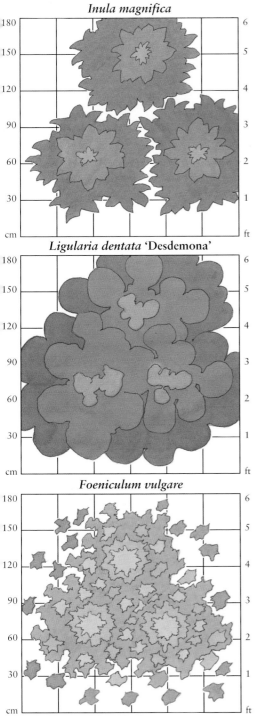

Inula magnifica

Ligularia dentata 'Desdemona'

Foeniculum vulgare

Inula magnifica

If you are looking for a plant to cheer you up in the late summer, this is the one. It forms large clumps of pointed oval leaves up to 2ft (60cm) long from which erect stems over 6ft (1.8m) tall rise during the summer. They are crowned by large flower heads about 6in (15cm) wide with numerous bright yellow, slender petals which give the plant a shaggy appearance. For a smaller garden, **Inula hookeri** grows to only 2ft (60cm) with 4in (10cm) leaves and light greeny-yellow flowers up to 4in (10cm) wide. Plant in well-drained, moisture-retentive soil.

z 3-9 sun or partial shade

Ligularia dentata 'Desdemona'

This clump-forming perennial is a majestic plant which introduces color and textural contrast to a border. The rounded, kidney-shaped basal leaves are up to 1ft (30cm) long, a dark green above and rich red-purple below. Bunches of up to 12 bright orange daisy-like flowers, 2½ to 5in (6.5-12.5cm) wide, are carried above rich red-purple stems, 3 to 4ft (90-120cm) tall, in late summer. **'The Rocket'** is another good cultivar of ligularia that has palmate leaves with dramatic dentations and tall racemes of pale yellow flowers. Grow in moisture-retentive soil.

z 4-8 sun or partial shade

Foeniculum vulgare

Fennel

Finely divided aromatic leaves emerge in spring, contrasting well with the foliage and flowers of other perennials and bulbs. The divided stems reach 6ft (1.8m) in summer with umbels of yellowish-green flowers that are followed by yellow seeds. It is advisable to cut the seed head before it ripens or you will have a large crop of seedlings; these must be weeded out as they have very strong taproots. The bronze-foliaged form, **purpureum**, is particularly attractive. Fennels do well in dry conditions.

z 4-10 sun

Macleaya (Bocconia) cordata   *Peltiphyllum peltatum*   *Delphinium* Pacific Hybrids

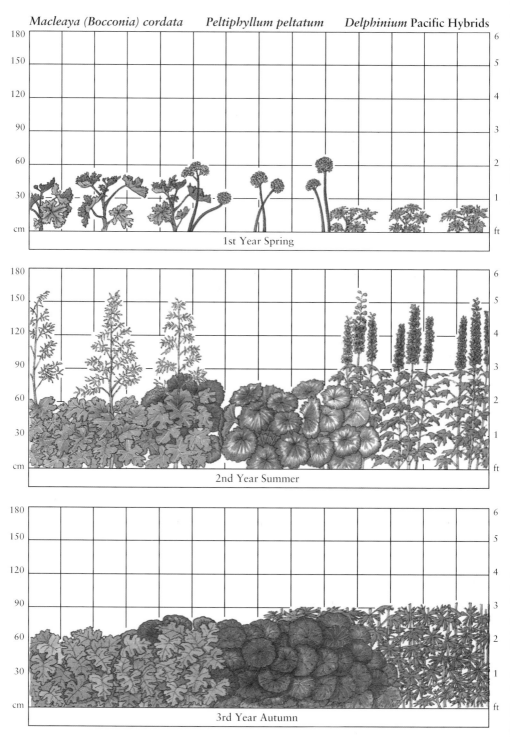

1st Year Spring

2nd Year Summer

3rd Year Autumn

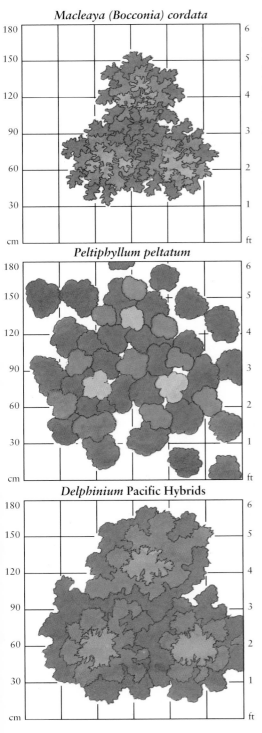

Macleaya (Bocconia) cordata

Both the foliage and the flowers of this plume poppy are admirable. The leaves have rounded lobes, are gray-green above, downy white below and up to 10in (25cm) long. The small white flowers are petalless and are carried in terminal panicles up to 7ft (2.1m) tall in late summer. This species is of slightly better quality than the more commonly found and more invasive **M. microcarpa**, which can grow up to 8ft (2.4m). This differs in having a freely running root system and rosy-buff flowers but it has equally beautiful foliage.

z 4-9 sun or partial shade

Peltiphyllum peltatum

Umbrella plant
In spring this plant has globe-like corymbs of delicate pink flowers held on otherwise bare red-tinted stems, 1 to 2ft (30-60cm) long. The stems arise from creeping rhizomes that resemble elephants' trunks. As the flowers fade colonies of deeply dissected leaves rapidly form. These are nearly circular, up to 1ft (30cm) in diameter, and are shiny green in summer, turning bright red with yellow veins in autumn. They give the plant a height of 3 to 4ft (90-120cm). Peltiphyllum needs moisture to succeed.

z 6-9 sun or partial shade

Delphinium Pacific Hybrids

Delphiniums grow into clumps up to 2ft (60cm) wide and produce stems of 4 to 6ft (1.2-1.8m) tall. The flowers are in vibrant tones of blue, white or purple, often with a contrasting eye, and give height to the early summer border. The pale green leaves are deeply lobed. They require deep, humus-rich, moisture-retentive soil and little disturbance. Among the common groups are the Pacific Hybrids and **Blue Fountains Series**. The latter are just 2ft (60cm) tall and require no staking. The red **University Hybrids** are sometimes available.

z 3-7 sun

Achillea filipendulina 'Gold Plate'   *Chrysanthemum maximum*   *Crocosmia* 'Lucifer'

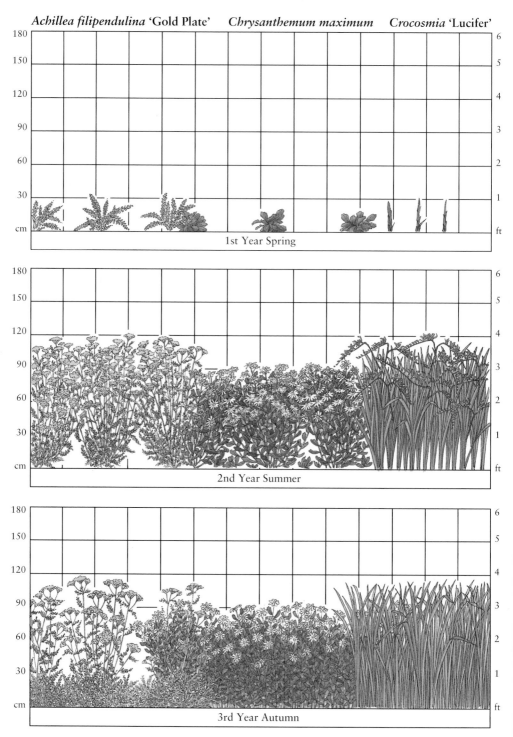

1st Year Spring

2nd Year Summer

3rd Year Autumn

160

Achillea filipendulina 'Gold Plate'

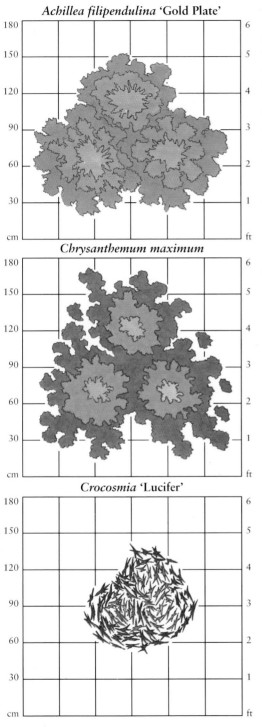

Achillea filipendulina 'Gold Plate'

Yarrow or milfoil

This strong plant has bold flat heads of tiny golden daisy flowers held on stiff stalks which reach 4ft (1.2m). The foliage is elegant and feathery and, if bruised, aromatic. '**Moonshine**' is shorter, has paler yellow flowers and grayer foliage. Other cultivars often found are '**Cerise Queen**', '**Red Beauty**' and '**The Pearl**' (white), but these are more floppy than 'Gold Plate'. All of these flower throughout the summer and thrive on well-drained soil of low fertility, spreading up to 3ft (90cm).

z 3-8 sun

Chrysanthemum maximum

Shasta daisy

This is one of the most reliable and brightest perennials. It is tolerant of most soils and quickly makes a clump that can easily be divided in late autumn or early spring. In most forms the flower stems grow to 2 or 3ft (60-90cm) with 3in (7.5cm) wide daisy blossoms that last well. If dead-headed, the plant will continue to flower through most of the summer. Cultivars include the double, frilly-petaled '**Aglaya**', pale yellow '**Cobham Gold**' and dwarf '**Snowcap**' that reaches 15in (37.5cm).

z 4-9 sun

Crocosmia 'Lucifer'

This delightful perennial is a large cultivar of montbretia, a cottage garden plant. The soft green tips of the sword-shaped foliage arise from corms which multiply steadily via tough rhizomes. The broad elegant leaves develop shallow pleats. Branched wiry stems up to 3ft (90cm) long carry flame red flowers 6in (15cm) or so long; these start to bloom in mid-summer and last up to four weeks. The pale yellow '**Solfatare**' and dark orange '**Emily McKenzie**' are two other good hybrids. Both grow to 2ft (60cm). All need moist soil.

z 5-8 sun or partial shade

161

Left: Yew, *Taxus baccata*, will quickly make a solid, formal, evergreen hedge that requires only one trim a year once it is established. Here a series of arches lead the visitor through successive garden rooms. Box edging clearly defines the path and accentuates the perspective.

Right: A low-growing, clipped yew hedge contrasts markedly with the billowy shape of the blue spruces. The architectural trellis-work is painted to complement the blue conifers.

Hedges

There are a great many trees and shrubs that can be used for hedging and each has different notable characteristics – evergreen or deciduous foliage, flowers or fruit – that make it appropriate for certain situations and styles of garden. Formal hedges need to be made of plants that respond to tight clipping, generating plenty of new shoots after being cut back. Informal hedges still need to be reasonably compact and graceful in shape.

There is considerable variation in growth rates. Some hedges will make an 8ft (2.4m) screen in six to eight years, or less. In order to keep such fast-growing hedges neat and at the chosen height, two or more cuts are needed each year. As pruning can be an arduous job, it might be better to select hedging plants that need only one cut a year. These may take a few more years to reach a satisfactory height, but they will be altogether less demanding than the vigorous growers.

Among the fastest-growing trees commonly used as a hedging plant is the Leyland cypress (× *Cupressocyparis leylandii*), closely followed by privet (*Ligustrum ovalifolium*) and the southern beech (*Nothofagus antarctica*). All three need up to three cuts a year, which must be started when the plants are young or they tend to become leggy and will not form a neat, dense screen. This is particularly important with the cypress which will not regenerate sufficient new shoots if cut only when it is mature.

Deciduous hedging plants are, as a rule, hardier than broad-leaved evergreens. The hawthorn *Crataegus monogyna* and some cherries are good deciduous plants, while hardy broad-leaved evergreens include *Prunus lusitanica* and *P. laurocerasus*. Among the hardiest plants suitable for hedging are some conifers, such as arborvitae (*Thuja occidentalis*), the western hemlock (*Tsuga heterophylla*) and its eastern counterpart (*T. canadensis*).

The longest-lived hedges are those of traditionally used species such as yew (*Taxus baccata*), beech (*Fagus sylvatica*) and box (*Buxus sempervirens*); it is possible to find hedges of these plants that are several centuries old. Even if the garden has been neglected and the hedges are overgrown or even derelict, it is often possible to prune the plants

back quite hard, preferably in spring, and promote young bushy growth.

Hedges are not difficult to grow, although following some simple guidelines can improve results.

First, the ground must be weed-free before planting. Treatment should begin during the preceding growing season. A systemic herbicide can be used on perennial weeds, ideally when they are growing most strongly. Once the ground is clean, add some organic matter, which will help retain moisture during dry periods, incorporating a slow-release fertilizer. The ground should be kept clear by frequent hoeing until planting. During the first few years of growth regular weeding should be

Left: Box, *Buxus sempervirens*, is a traditional hedging plant, excellently suited to create a parterre. It will reach 8 to 12in (20-30cm) fairly quickly and thereafter requires only one clip a year. Its small leaves and tight character make it ideal for topiary specimens, although complicated forms take ten to 20 years to achieve.

Below: There are a range of cypresses that make fast-growing hedges. They should be tightly clipped up the sides at least twice a year from the second or third year on, as few young shoots will grow following a severe cut. This is *Cupressus macrocarpa* 'Golden Cone'.

grown specimens. The cheapest are bare-rooted deciduous species, which need to be planted during the dormant season. Evergreens are often sold in containers and can be planted at most times of the year, although early autumn or late spring are preferable. Container-grown plants, however, are costly and it is worth seeking out a nursery that can supply these plants bare-rooted.

Each hedge will require slightly different treatment when it comes to pruning, although there are some general principles to follow. The aim is to create a strong framework with plenty of lateral growth all the way down to the ground. There are at least two

undertaken, to minimize competition.

Alternatively, the ground can be covered with black plastic sheeting for a year before planting (after organic matter has been added). The hedging plants are inserted through slits made in the plastic, which should only be cut away when the plants are mature (although it is likely to deteriorate before then). This technique is unsightly but effective and is favored by those who do not like using chemicals. Remember that rain will not penetrate through the plastic so additional watering will probably be necessary.

It is possible to purchase hedging plants in three forms: bare-rooted, root-balled and burlapped, or as container-

Left: *Rosa rugosa* makes an impenetrable 6 to 7ft (1.8-2.1m) informal hedge in just a few years. It is attractive throughout the summer and into autumn, as the flowers are followed by deep red hips that are set off by the golden yellow autumn foliage.

Below: Topiary specimens bring a strong architectural quality to a garden. Holly can be slow growing but will make a solid glossy mass. Here it has been cut into dumpy bollards, 5ft (1.5m) high, which contrast with the soaring points of the yew cones in the background.

schools of thought on how to achieve this, but I favor letting the leader grow to the desired height of the hedge, particularly with a coniferous hedge. Side shoots should be trimmed back to about 6in (15cm) inside the ultimate width of the hedge. There should be no long shoots between the plants as these tend to be weak and straggly. In the formative years it may be necessary to trim the plants two or three times in the season, particularly strong-growing species. Pruning should give the hedge a "batter", a sloping surface, rather narrower at the top than at the base. This ensures that the base receives sufficient light to grow strongly.

Once the hedge is dense enough it can be maintained with one or two cuts per year. Generally speaking, spring is the best time to prune deciduous species, just as growth begins. However, in their early years, hornbeam (*Carpinus betulus*) and beech (*Fagus sylvatica*), produce soft growth which should be shortened in late spring or early summer if the hedge is to retain its compact quality. When these species are mature a late summer or early autumn trim will cause them to keep their leaves for much longer in the winter.

The best time to prune flowering hedges depends on when they are in bloom. Those that flower early in the season, on the previous year's growth, should be trimmed immediately after

flowering in late spring or early summer. Hedges that flower later in the season, on the current year's wood, should be cut back in early spring to encourage the production of plenty of strong, new, flowering stems.

Evergreen hedges do best with a late summer trim unless the climate is very hard, in which case early spring is best. Fast-growers such as privet, *Lonicera nitida* and Leyland cypress can be trimmed in spring and then again in mid- and late summer.

It may be necessary to erect a temporary screen while the hedge is growing to protect it from the wind and cold or to hide an ugly view outside the garden. A trellis panel backing the hedge may be sufficient, although a more substantial effect is achieved by enclosing the hedge within trellis panels. The plants can be trimmed to the size of the box which will eventually rot away. As an alternative, green burlap stretched against green-stained trellis will protect the plants in winter and provide privacy in the garden.

THE GROWTH CHARTS
The following pruning codes are used:
✱: prune in winter.
◗: prune in spring.
✚: prune in summer.
❖: prune in late summer.
■: prune hard back in late winter or early spring to improve flowering.
●: prune soon after flowering ends.

Berberis thunbergii

This barberry has outstanding autumn foliage color and will make a dense hedge 5ft (1.5m) high in ten years. It has small deciduous leaves, bright green above and gray beneath. The tiny red flowers are followed by bead-like shiny red fruit. In winter the bark stands out reddish-brown. Its form *atropurpurea*, which is perhaps the hardiest of the barberries, is taller, reaching 6ft (1.8m), and has deep bronze leaves in the spring and summer, turning purple in the autumn. Plant both varieties at 18in (45cm) intervals.

z 4-8 sun or shade u.h. 6ft (1.8m) ■

Buxus sempervirens

Common box

A small round-leaved evergreen shrub which grows slowly, reaching barely 4ft (1.2m) in ten years. It stands severe pruning so is ideal for topiary. The variety **'Suffruticosa'** has smaller leaves and is better suited for edging. Box copes with most soils if the climate is not too harsh but it prefers good drainage. As a shrub or small tree it will reach 10ft (3m). The dwarf, shrubby germander **Teucrium chamaedrys**, which has shiny dark green leaves, can be used for edging and parterres in very cold areas.

z 7-9 sun or shade u.h. 8ft (2.4m) ✿/◗

Crataegus monogyna

Common hawthorn

A traditional deciduous hedgerow plant that makes a tight 8ft (2.4m) screen in less than ten years but is, regrettably, not frequently used in gardens. The dense twiggy growth is covered with small white to pale pink fragrant flowers in mid- to late spring, followed by pale green leaves. It is best pruned in summer, but if you want to see the autumn berries it can be pruned every other year. Mix with privet, hazel, field maple, hornbeam or beech. Plant at 1ft (30cm) intervals; prune back to 1ft (30cm) after planting.

z 4-7 sun or partial shade u.h. 20ft (6m) ●✻

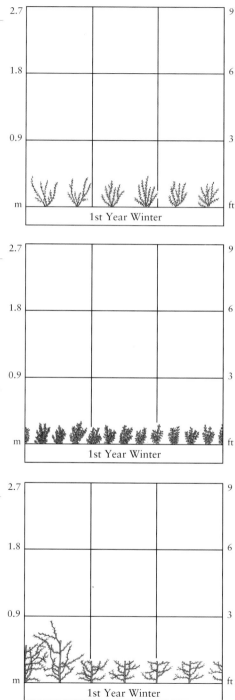

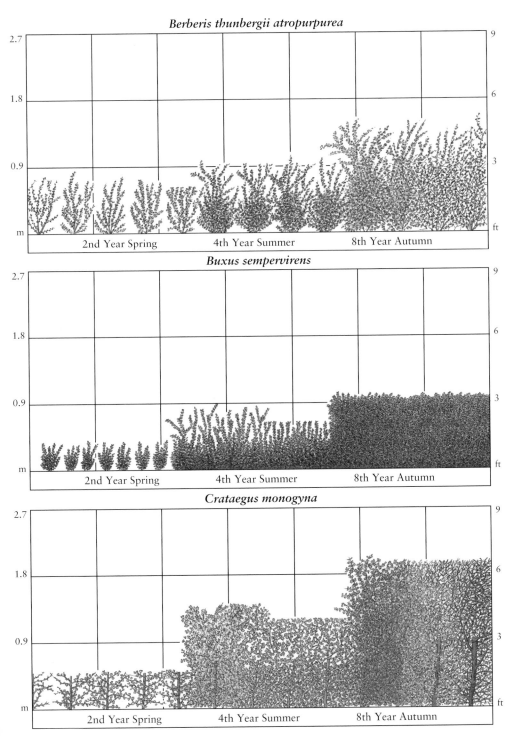

Berberis thunbergii atropurpurea

2nd Year Spring   4th Year Summer   8th Year Autumn

Buxus sempervirens

2nd Year Spring   4th Year Summer   8th Year Autumn

Crataegus monogyna

2nd Year Spring   4th Year Summer   8th Year Autumn

Elaeagnus macrophylla

An excellent hedge in under ten years, reaching 10ft (3m), spreading more than 6ft (1.8m). It is a better plant than the more commonly seen, hardier *E.* × *ebbingei* or *E. pungens* and its gold-variegated cultivar **'Aurea'** which have smaller leaves. All are evergreen and *E. macrophylla* has large leathery gray-green leaves, silver-backed and with wavy edges. Mature plants bear small white fragrant flowers in autumn on the old wood. All these plants are best pruned in late summer with hand pruners. Plant at 3ft (90cm) intervals.

z 6-9 sun or partial shade u.h. 10ft (3m) ◗

Euonymus alatus

Burning bush

This spindle has a loose habit but withstands hard pruning and makes a hedge 6ft (1.8m) tall in less than ten years. Its chief glory is its bright pinkish autumn foliage which is all the more striking if the plant has good drainage. The fruit is purple and the angled stems develop corky outgrowths as the plant matures. The cultivar **'Compactus'** is denser and reaches only 4ft (1.2m) in ten years. The evergreen *E. japonicus* is more tender but thrives by the sea and reaches 6ft (1.8m). Plant at 2ft (60cm) intervals.

z 3-9 sun or partial shade u.h. 6ft (1.8m) ✳

Fagus sylvatica

Common beech

Unlike the similar hornbeam (*Carpinus betulus*), beech does not tolerate damp, cold conditions and grows best on a well-drained (sandy or chalky) soil. It is susceptible to late spring frosts so needs shelter to achieve 8ft (2.4m) in ten years. The deciduous leaves are larger and smoother than hornbeam and remain throughout the winter, especially if pruned late in the season. Copper beech is a colorful alternative. Plant 18 to 24in (45-60cm) apart or every 24in (60cm) in two staggered rows 8in (20cm) apart.

z 4-8 sun or partial shade u.h 10ft (3m) ❖

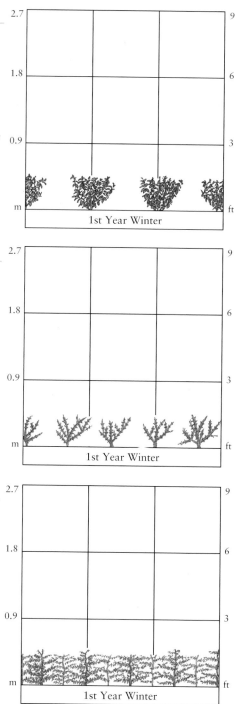

2.7 / 1.8 / 0.9 / m — 9 / 6 / 3 / ft
1st Year Winter

2.7 / 1.8 / 0.9 / m — 9 / 6 / 3 / ft
1st Year Winter

2.7 / 1.8 / 0.9 / m — 9 / 6 / 3 / ft
1st Year Winter

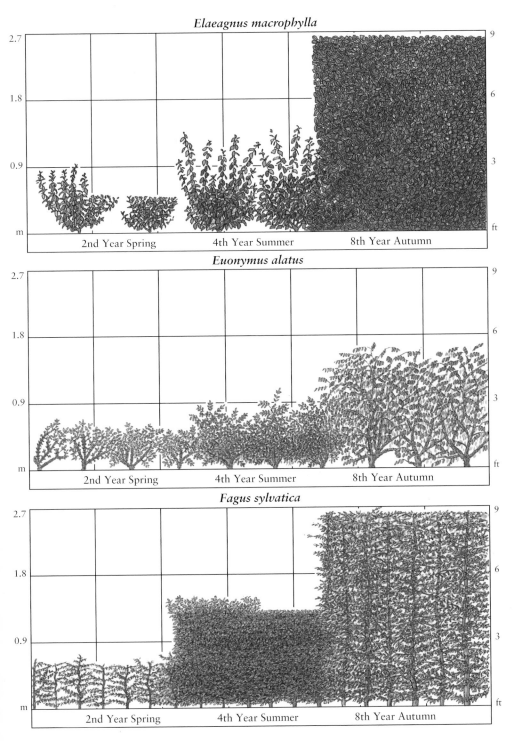

Elaeagnus macrophylla

2nd Year Spring   4th Year Summer   8th Year Autumn

Euonymus alatus

2nd Year Spring   4th Year Summer   8th Year Autumn

Fagus sylvatica

2nd Year Spring   4th Year Summer   8th Year Autumn

Hippophae rhamnoides

Sea buckthorn

A tough wind-resistant shrub that can be used to create a screen 12ft (3.6m) high in ten years in inhospitable conditions. It tolerates sandy dry soils, salt air and pollution. The stiff, thorny branches bear deciduous narrow gray-green leaves. The tiny clusters of petalless flowers are followed in late summer by an abundance of bright orange berries that remain on the plant throughout the winter. Plants are dioecious so for reliable berrying at least one male to six female plants must be used. Plant 2 to 3ft (60-90cm) apart.

z 3-8 sun or partial shade u.h. 15ft (4.5m) ◗/✱

Ilex aquifolium

Hollies make excellent dense hedges. The English holly, *I. aquifolium*, barely reaches 5ft (1.5m) in ten years; the American holly, *I. opaca*, reaches 7 to 8ft (2.1-2.4m), withstanding long, hot and humid summers. The blue hollies are the most cold-resistant: *I. × merserveae*, and the deciduous *I. verticillata*. They have spiny, shiny green leaves, with different kinds of variegation. Small white flowers hide at the base of the leaves in summer. Female forms need a male pollinator to produce berries. *I. aquifolium* 'Golden Queen' is male. Plant 2ft (60cm) apart.

z 4-9 sun or shade u.h. 10ft (3m) ◗/❖

Ligustrum ovalifolium 'Aureum'

Golden privet

Privet is a fast-growing hedge that may require two to three cuts in a season. The golden form is slightly slower-growing, reaching 8ft (2.4m) in six to eight years. It has sunny gold leaves; any branches reverting to plain green should be cut out immediately as they grow more vigorously and will quickly take over. Prune in late spring and again in summer. For colder areas the green *L. amurense*, *L. obtusifolium* or *L. vulgaris* 'Cheyenne' and the golden *L. vulgaris* 'Aureum' are hardier. Plant at 2ft (60cm) intervals.

z 5-9 sun or partial shade u.h. 12ft (3.6m) ◗❖

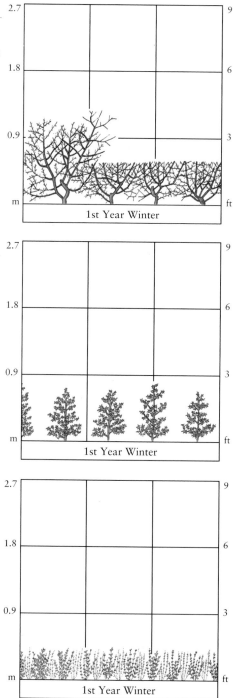

1st Year Winter

1st Year Winter

1st Year Winter

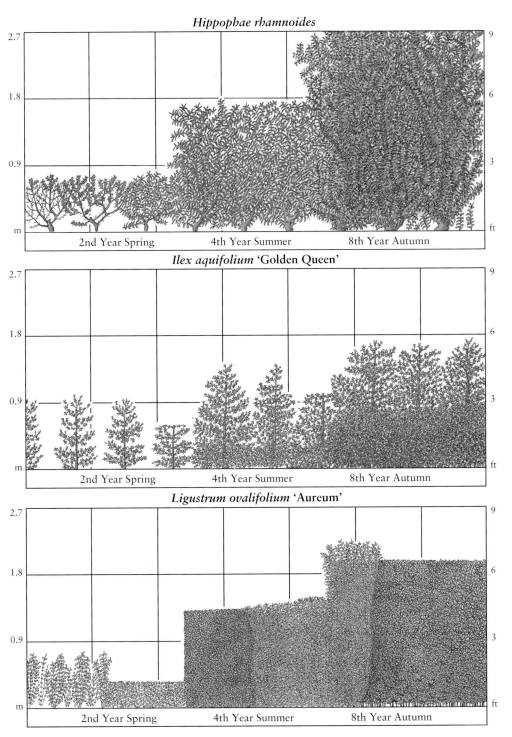

Hippophae rhamnoides

2.7 — 9
1.8 — 6
0.9 — 3
m — ft

2nd Year Spring   4th Year Summer   8th Year Autumn

Ilex aquifolium 'Golden Queen'

2.7 — 9
1.8 — 6
0.9 — 3
m — ft

2nd Year Spring   4th Year Summer   8th Year Autumn

Ligustrum ovalifolium 'Aureum'

2.7 — 9
1.8 — 6
0.9 — 3
m — ft

2nd Year Spring   4th Year Summer   8th Year Autumn

Lonicera nitida

This evergreen shrubby honeysuckle has stiff twiggy branches tightly clothed with tiny glossy green leaves. It will reach 5ft (1.5m) but needs regular clipping in a wedge shape or it can develop bare patches. A leggy hedge can be cut right back in early spring. **'Baggessen's Gold'** has golden leaves all summer that turn greenish-yellow in the autumn. *L. pileata* is similar in foliage but much smaller in height, making it ideal for edging. The deciduous *L. tatarica* is much hardier. Plant at 1ft (30cm) intervals and prune back to 1ft (30cm).

z 7-10 sun or shade u.h. 5ft (1.5m) ▶✿

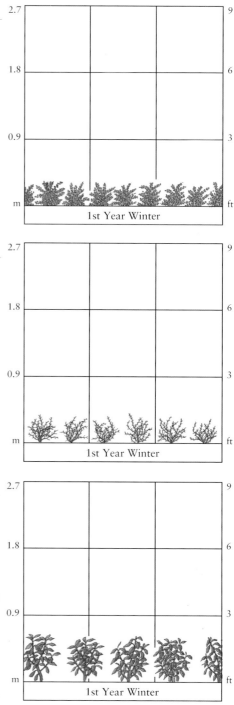

Potentilla fruticosa 'Goldfinger'

Cinquefoil

A dense informal hedge, attractive from early summer to the autumn. The rounded habit grows to 5ft (1.5m) in ten years. It is adaptable to most soil conditions and is extremely hardy. The small deciduous pinnate leaves are a dense green and the plentiful five-petaled flowers deep yellow. **'Katherine Dykes'** (pale yellow) and **'Farrer's White'** (white) grow to about the same height as 'Goldfinger', while **'Red Ace'** (vermilion) reaches only 20 to 30in (50-75cm). Plant 18in (45cm) apart. Prune in early spring.

z 2-8 sun u.h. 5ft (1.5m) ■

Prunus lusitanica

Portugal laurel

A handsome evergreen with shiny, dark green, oval leaves on red stems. It is happy in most soils, even shallow and alkaline ones, reaching 6ft (1.8m) in ten years. Although it withstands hard pruning, racemes of white flowers will only blossom in early summer if the hedge is left to grow informally. The deciduous downy cherry, *P. tomentosa*, is much hardier and in spring is covered with white blossom. The leaves are dark dull green and after a hot summer bright red fruits abound. Plant 2ft (60cm) apart.

z 7-9 sun or partial shade u.h. 15ft (4.5m) ▶✚

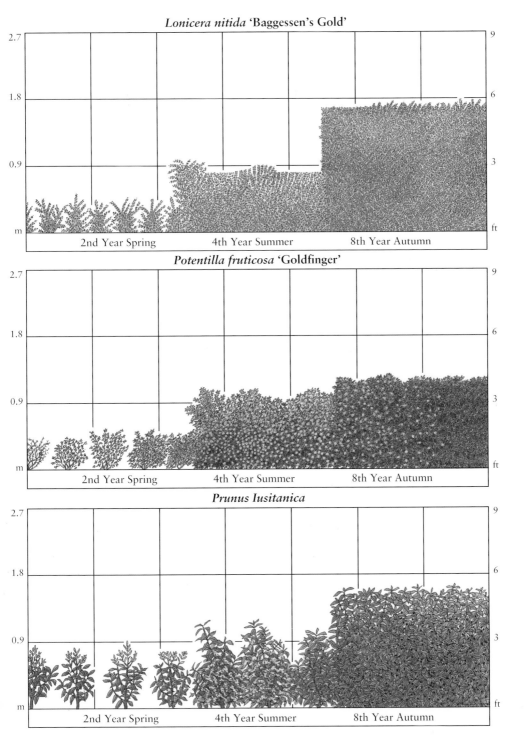

Lonicera nitida 'Baggessen's Gold'

2nd Year Spring   4th Year Summer   8th Year Autumn

Potentilla fruticosa 'Goldfinger'

2nd Year Spring   4th Year Summer   8th Year Autumn

Prunus lusitanica

2nd Year Spring   4th Year Summer   8th Year Autumn

Rosa rugosa

One of the most rugged of shrub-roses, resistant to most diseases, this plant grows quickly to make a compact, dense and prickly hedge up to 5ft (1.5m) high. The stout stems are clothed in apple green leaves that turn yellow in the autumn. Bright red hips, 1in (2.5cm) around and flattened at the top, follow the fragrant flowers which are deep pink in the species. 'Alba' has pure white flowers with yellow stamens; 'Fru Dagmar Hastrup' has clear pink flowers; 'Roseraie de l'Haÿ' has double crimson flowers but no hips. Plant 3ft (90cm) apart.

z 3-8 sun u.h. 5ft (1.5m) ■

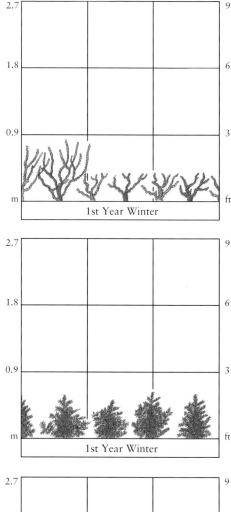

1st Year Winter

Taxus baccata

Yew

A remarkable evergreen, equally happy in acid and alkaline soils, sun or shade. With an annual top dressing of fertilizer, yew will grow quite rapidly, reaching 8ft (2.4m) in ten years. Both the leaves and seeds (protected by a fleshy red aril) are poisonous. The species has black-green foliage but there are several attractive golden forms. The hybrid cultivar *T. × media* 'Hicksii' is more consistently hardy and able to withstand lower temperatures. Both are suitable for topiary. Plant 2ft (60cm) apart. Trim in late summer.

z 6-8 sun or shade u.h. 15ft (4.5m) ❖

1st Year Winter

Thuja occidentalis

American arborvitae

This very hardy species tolerates cold conditions and wet soils. It can reach 10ft (3m) in ten years. The evergreen foliage is bright green in spring and turns duller through the season. The western red cedar, *T. plicata*, is less hardy but faster growing. It reaches 10ft (3m) in eight years, if protected from frost and drought early on, although it will tolerate highly alkaline and dry conditions once it is well established. Trim both plants in late summer. Plant at 2ft (60cm) intervals.

z 3-8 sun u.h. 12ft (3.6m) ❖

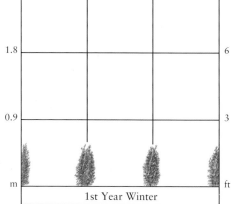

1st Year Winter

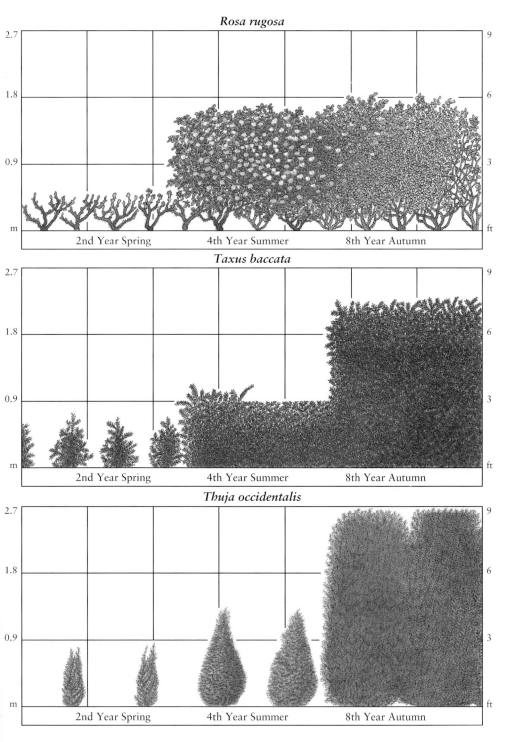

Rosa rugosa

Taxus baccata

Thuja occidentalis

Right: The early to mid-summer lily 'Connecticut King' is just one of many hybrids available. These fleshy-scaled bulbous plants need plenty of moisture and sunshine but survive for longest in well-drained soil.

Far right, top: In early spring the delicate flowers of *Cyclamen coum* emerge from shallow-planted corms, amid a sea of attractively marked leaves. Snowdrop bulbs are planted somewhat deeper. Both need cool conditions, partial shade and moisture-rententive soil.
Far right, bottom: *Erythronium revolutum* produce perennial tubers which spread rapidly, forming clumps of heart-shaped, mottled leaves and in mid- to late spring deep to pale pink flowers. They like partial shade and moist, well-drained soil.

Bulbs

It is possible to have bulbs flowering in the garden every day of the year. Broadly speaking, those most frequently found in cultivation in temperate gardens grow and flower from autumn through the winter until late spring. Most species, both hardy (to zone 6) and tender (zones 9 and 10), originate from areas of the world with a Mediterranean-type climate; that is, hot, dry summers and cool, wet winters. These include the coastal regions around the Mediterranean Sea, the west coast of the United States from Oregon to south California, the Cape of South Africa, southern Chile, and western and south Australia.

Species that flower in the summer come from areas where the growing season is hot and rainy and the winter (or dormant period) is dry and cool. This type of climate is found in tropical and subtropical areas of both central and southern Africa, and North and South America. These are all tender and require hothouse conditions to grow outside their natural habitat.

There are three main bulbous families, the iris family (Iridaceae), the daffodil family (Amaryllidaceae) and the lily family (Liliaceae). These account for most of the ornamental genera that are grown in gardens.

The cultivation of bulbs is not difficult providing the dry resting period, to which most species are adapted, is respected.

Tender bulbs such as *Hymenocallis*, *Chlidanthus*, *Agapanthus*, *Clivia* and *Lachenalia* are striking grown in pots but must have frost-free conditions in winter. They multiply steadily and need repotting when the pot is quite full but not before as they mostly thrive in restricted conditions. Plenty of water is necessary as they start into growth and when they are in flower. As the flowers fade, additional feeding will ensure that the bulb builds up enough reserves to survive the resting period. Other tender bulbs are suitable for planting out in spring after frosts have passed and are particularly useful for filling spaces that appear in herbaceous borders. These include many of the *Gladiolus* species, *Ixia viridiflora* and *Tigridia pavonia* (peacock or tiger flower). To save the bulbs for the following year, lift them in the late autumn and store in dry, frost-free conditions until the spring.

179

Hardy bulbs are easier to grow in the garden as they do not need lifting. Once they are established they will increase steadily, making a stunning display annually. Many species, including daffodils (*Narcissus* spp.), *Crocus vernus*, *Crocus tommasinianus*, *Leucojum aestivum* (summer snowflake), *Fritillaria meleagris* (snake's-head fritillary) and *Ornithogalum nutans* (star-of-Bethlehem), can be naturalized in rough grass. The trick here is to ensure that the flowers rise above the grass and that the plants remain in leaf for some time, to ensure that a flower bud is formed within the bulb for the following season. For example, daffodils need to keep their leaves for approximately six weeks after they finish flowering before

they are cut back. Hardy bulbs also look at home in deciduous woodland as they flower before the trees' leaf canopies have filled out. Daffodils, trilliums, snowdrops, cyclamens, bluebells, erythroniums, winter aconites and some lilies are most successful in wooded areas.

Winter aconites bloom from winter to early spring, as do snowdrops. Cyclamen are in flower between late autumn and winter, while a number of irises give winter flowers, including *I. stylosa* (early winter) and *I. danfordiae* and *I. reticulata* (mid- to late winter).

If bulbs are to be grown in a true herbaceous border they will need to be planted very deep so that they are not disturbed by weeding or by digging to lift and divide plants. It is easier to associate them with deep-rooted perennials that do not require regular lifting and splitting: for example, English ivy, *Inula helenium* (elecampane), and some of the densely leaved hardy geraniums (cranesbills), hostas, peonies and alchemillas, provide perfect carpets for bulbs which emerge in the spring. As the bulbs fade they are covered by the herbaceous leaves which will have entered their growing season.

In mixed borders bulbs can be most effective growing under spring-flowering trees or shrubs and look well with evergreen ground cover.

Tulips and hyacinths are often grown with spring bedding plants as they are reliable and put on a bright show. They can be lifted at the same time as the bedding plants but some soil should be kept around the roots to prevent them from being damaged. The bulbs should then be put into a box to dry. When they have dried off they can be cleaned, dusted with fungicide, and stored until the autumn in a dry, well-ventilated area.

There are many dwarf bulbs that thrive in rock gardens or peat beds. They require sharp drainage so should be planted in a fertile soil containing a high proportion of leaf mold or other well-rotted vegetable matter, mixed with grit, in a ratio of roughly two parts soil to one of grit. Dwarf narcissi, tulips, scillas, chionodoxas, fritillaries, paris and trilliums are just a few of the species that are suitable.

Left: In a warm position the late *Narcissus* 'Hawera' blossoms with the early *Tulipa bakeri* 'Lilac Wonder'. Both these bulbous species require a good summer baking to complete their annual growth cycle.
Below: *Allium moly* is a small member of the onion family, some 4 to 5in (10-12cm) high. It requires dry, sharply draining soil and produces clumps of gray-green leaves and umbels of yellow flowers in summer.

Right: French marigolds and begonias are traditionally used for formal bedding. Here a central bed of dwarf begonias and silver-leaved dusty miller (*Cineraria maritima*) is surrounded by raised beds of yellow and orange marigolds, trimmed by the blue spikes of salvia.

Annuals and biennials

Far right: The white foxglove, *Digitalis purpurea alba*, and the cotton or Scotch thistle, *Onopordum acanthium*, are biennials that self-seed in flower gardens. In the first year they make bold rosettes of basal foliage from which the flower spikes grow up in the second year.

Annuals and biennials can be great allies of the gardener. They fill empty spaces very rapidly and can be used en masse as bedding plants or scattered among perennials and shrubs. They are also ideally suited to hanging baskets, tubs and window boxes. They give life and color to the first year of a new garden and help the owner become acquainted with the site. Their transitory nature is a positive advantage: it allows for trial and error in planting schemes, the unsuccessful design of one year being corrected in the next. When a satisfactory combination of colors and heights has been found using annuals and biennials, a similar scheme can be created with confidence, using long-lasting perennials.

Annuals and biennials are easy to grow, which makes them an asset in any planting scheme. They offer a wealth of colors and vary widely in height, from tiny dwarf, compact forms of *ageratum* (floss flowers) for neat edgings, to great sunflowers that make a screen from summer to autumn.

Biennials differ from annuals in that their life cycle is spread over two years. In the first year they produce basal leaves that usually overwinter as a rosette, a ground-hugging cluster of leaves. The flower spike is produced in the second growing season, after which the plant sets seed and dies. The most frequently found self-seeding biennials are *Digitalis purpurea* (foxglove) and *Lunaria* (honesty), but there are many others, including *Onopordum giganteum* (giant thistle) and *Eryngium giganteum* (Miss Willmott's ghost). Some of the most popular bedding plants are biennials but these are best grown annually from seed.

Annuals are generally divided into hardy and half-hardy varieties. The sowing time of hardy types, such as *Amaranthus caudatus* (love-lies-bleeding), is not crucial: provided the soil is not too wet or the weather too frosty, they can be sown in succession from early spring until summer to ensure flowering from summer well into autumn. A few hardy annuals, such as *Centaurea cyanus* (cornflower) and *Calendula officinalis* (pot marigold), can be sown (or self-seed) in late summer and will overwinter as rosettes before flowering in late spring or early summer. Most hardy annuals need

minimal thinning to succeed. Spring-flowering biennials, such as the attractive *Bellis perennis* (double daisy), *Myosotis* (forget-me-not) and *Cheiranthus* (wallflower), should be sown in pots in summer and transplanted in the autumn to their flowering positions. Summer-flowering biennials, such as *Papaver nudicaule* (Iceland poppy), *Matthiola incana* (Brompton stock) and *Dianthus barbatus* (sweet William), can be sown in late summer, thinned in autumn and

transplanted to their flowering positions in spring.

Some half-hardy annuals can be raised outdoors without too much difficulty. These useful plants include *Tagetes patula* (French marigold), *Matthiola* (stock), *Antirrhinum* (snapdragon) and *Helichrysum bracteatum* (everlasting flower). However, most – including begonias, calceolarias, dahlias, petunias, lobelias, cosmos and *Tagetes erecta* (African marigold) – should be sown indoors in early spring, in a propagator in a greenhouse, or more simply in pots on a window ledge inside the house. It is important that night and day temperatures do not vary too wildly and that the seedlings do not dry out in direct sunlight. Once the seedlings are large enough to handle they need to be

pricked out, the strongest seedlings being carefully transplanted into a new container with sufficient space for them to develop unhindered. When any risk of frost has passed and the seedlings are sufficiently mature (and after a period of hardening off in a cold frame or a sheltered spot in the garden) they can be planted out.

If raising seedlings is too time-consuming and takes up too much space, the alternative is to purchase seedlings direct from garden centers or catalogs. If you are able to select your own plants, always look out for plump, green, healthy seedlings that are not showing signs of wilt, pests or diseases, and have a minimum of roots showing through the container walls.

All annuals do best in a reasonably sunny and open space and require good soil to flower throughout the summer. Poor soil results in small plants that flower early, set seed, and die before the end of the summer. As with all other plants, weeding is necessary in the early stages, but once plants are established and begin to grow they will suppress most surrounding weeds.

Watering is most important when the seedlings are establishing themselves. Thereafter, water only if conditions are very dry or if the plants are being grown in containers. In such cases, a good soak at fairly long intervals is better than frequent, superficial watering. Provided the soil is fertile, little

The choice of colors in a bed of annuals is an important consideration. Here are two coordinating schemes in shades of pink.
Far left: Impatiens, white petunias, statice (*Psylliostachis suworowii*) and cosmos 'Sensation' make a bold splash from mid-summer onwards.
Left: *Amaranthus caudatus* and *Lavatera trimestris* 'Silver Cup' stand high beyond the lower-growing *Silene coeli-rosa* 'Rose Angel'.

additional feeding is necessary, except for container-grown plants; a weekly dose of liquid feed will ensure that they thrive throughout the summer.

Many varieties of annuals and biennials are bred for their compact characteristics, including verbenas, French marigolds, coreopsis and dahlias (all of which are annuals), *Campanula medium* (Canterbury bell), wallflowers and sweet Williams (all biennials). However, it is often necessary to pinch ends back before flowering starts, to encourage bushiness. Straggly stems should be pruned back, which in turn will encourage new strong growth. Once flowering begins, regular dead-heading will not only enhance a plant's appearance but will also extend the flowering period. Little other attention needs to be given to these useful plants, although taller annuals, such as sunflowers, may need some kind of support to brace them against strong winds.

When annuals have died back and biennials have completed their life cycle, dig them up, discard onto the compost heap and refresh the soil with well-rotted organic matter. It is a good idea to make a note of the most successful species for future use – as well as the disappointing plants, to be avoided.

Glossary

Terms in italics cross-refer to other glossary entries.

Acid Describes a soil with a *pH* of below 7.

Aerial root A root that emerges from the stem of a plant above ground level.

Alkaline Describes a soil with a *pH* over 7.

Alternate leaves, buds, stems These occur singly on stems, alternating from one side to the other.

Annual A plant that completes its life cycle within one growing season.

Aril A covering on some seeds that is often brightly colored and fleshy.

Basal foliage The foliage nearest the base of a plant.

Biennial A plant that produces roots, stems and leaves in the first growing season and flowers in the second, at the end of which it dies.

Bipinnate Describes *pinnate* leaves arranged on opposite sides of a stalk.

Bract A modified leaf at the base of the flower head, either reduced or scale-like or large and brightly colored.

Calyx The *whorl* of leaf-like sepals surrounding a flower.

Catkin A hanging cluster of much reduced flowers.

Choice see *Tender*

Clone A plant identical to the parent plant, raised by vegetative *propagation* (by division, layering, grafting or taking cuttings).

Corymb A flat-topped flower cluster.

Crenate Desribes a leaf with a scalloped edge.

Cultivar Short for cultivated variety, an identified variation of a *species*.

Deciduous Used mainly to describe trees and shrubs that lose all their leaves at the end of the growing season, usually in autumn.

Dentate Describes a leaf with a toothed edge.

Digitate Describes a compound leaf that resembles a spread hand.

Dioecious Plants that bear either male or female flowers, not both.

Evergreen A plant, usually a tree or a shrub, that keeps its foliage for at least a year.

Floret A single flower in a head of a number of flowers.

Glaucous Describes stems covered with a bluish, powdery or waxy bloom.

Habit The natural mode of growth of a plant.

Herbaceous Describes a *perennial* plant that dies back to the ground level at the end of the growing season.

Humus Fertile, decayed organic matter.

Hybrid A plant produced by crossing two distinct parents. These can be members of different genera, two *species* within a genus, or *varieties* within a species. A hybrid is usually denoted by a multiplication sign (×) within the Latin name.

Inflorescence The arrangement of flowers on a stalk.

Key A winged seed.

Lanceolate Describes a narrow, tapering leaf.

Leader The dominant, usually uppermost shoot in a stem system.

Microclimate A climate particular to a specific situation (for example, a sheltered corner of a garden) which differs from the overall climate of the area.

Mulch A layer of organic matter or an inorganic material (plastic or gravel) applied over or around a plant, that can protect the plant from cold in winter, reduce evaporation in summer, suppress weeds and, with an organic mulch, will enrich the soil.

Mushroom compost The spent compost in which mushrooms have been grown commercially.

Obovate Describes a leaf that is inversely *ovate*, with the narrower end at the base.

Ovate Describes a leaf shaped like the longitudinal section of an egg, with the broader end at the base.

Palmate Describes a leaf with five lobes arising from a common point.

Panicle A branched *raceme*.

Perennial A plant that lives for at least three years.

Petiole The stalk of a leaf.

pH The scale by which acidity or alkalinity is measured.

Pinnate Describes a leaf that is composed of paired leaflets along a stalk.

Procumbent Growing along the ground.

Propagation The production of a new plant from an existing one, either sexually, by seeds, or vegetatively, for example by cuttings.

Prostrate see *Procumbent*

Raceme An *inflorescence* in which the flowers are borne along the main stem, singly or in small clusters.

Rain shadow An area of ground shielded from the rain by the eaves of a roof or by the dense leaf canopy of a tree or a shrub.

Rhizome A horizontal underground stem that acts as a storage organ.

Runner A rooting stem that grows along the surface of the soil.

Sharply draining soil Soil that rapidly drains of excess water.

Shrub A perennial plant with several woody stems branching from the base. Plants with soft upper shoots that usually die in winter are termed sub-shrubs.

Species A group of closely related plants within a genus.

Specimen A plant grown on its own, independent of a planting scheme; usually applied to trees and shrubs.

Spike A *raceme* of stalkless flowers.

Stolon A stem which grows horizontally, usually above ground, and roots at its tip to form a new plant.

Systemic herbicide, fungicide or insecticide Chemicals which permeate an entire plant and kill certain diseases or parasitic insects.

Taproot The main, vertical root of a plant, or any strong, vertical root.

Tender Describes any plant

likely to be damaged by low temperatures.
Terminal bud, shoot, panicle The uppermost growth on a stem.
Trace elements Various essential chemical elements, required by plants in very small quantities.
Trifoliate Having three leaves, or three leaflets.
Truss A compact cluster of flowers or fruit.
Umbel A rounded or flat cluster of flowers, in which each flower stalk arises from the same point on the main stem. In a compound umbel each stalk bears an umbel.
Variegated Describes leaves with colored markings.
Variety A distinct form of a species.
Whorl An arrangement of three or more leaves, shoots or flowers around a stem.

Bibliography

Bailey, L.H. and E.Z., *Hortus Third*, 3rd edition, Macmillan, New York, 1976

Bean, W.G., *Trees and Shrubs Hardy in the British Isles*, 8th edition, John Murray, London, 1988

Beckett, Kenneth A., *Climbing Plants*, Croom Helm, London, 1983

Beckett, Kenneth A., *The Concise Encyclopedia of Garden Plants*, Orbis, London, 1983

Boisset, Caroline, *Vertical Gardening*, Mitchell Beazley, London, Grove/Weidenfeld and Nicolson, New York, 1988

Boisset, Caroline, *Gardening in Time*, Mitchell Beazley, London, Prentice-Hall, New Jersey, 1990

Clausen, R.R. and Ekstrom, N.H., *Perennials for American Gardens*, Random House, New York, 1989

Evison, Raymond J., *Making the Most of Clematis*, Floraprint, Wisbech, 1987

Grey-Wilson, C. and Matthews, V., *Gardening on Walls*, Harper Collins, London, 1983

Joyce, David, *Pruning and Training Plants*, Mitchell Beazley, London, Simon and Schuster, New York, 1992

Lloyd, Christopher, *Clematis*, Harper Collins, London, 1989

Phillips, Roger and Rix, Martyn, *Bulbs*, Pan Books, London, Random House, New York, 1989

Phillips, Roger and Rix, Martyn, *Roses*, Pan Books, London, Random House, New York, 1988

Phillips, Roger and Rix, Martyn, *Shrubs*, Pan Books, London, Random House, New York, 1989

Rose, Peter Q., *Climbers and Wall Plants*, Blandford Press, London, 1982

Rose, Peter Q., *Ivies*, Blandford Press, London, 1980

Royal Horticultural Society, *Dictionary of Gardening*, 2nd edition, Clarendon Press, Oxford, 1986

Royal Horticultural Society, editor-in-chief Christopher Brickell, *Gardeners' Encyclopedia of Plants and Flowers*, Dorling Kindersley, London, 1989; published as *The American Horticultural Society's Encyclopedia of Garden Plants*, Macmillan, New York, 1989

Royal Horticultural Society's Encyclopedia of Practical Gardening, editor-in-chief Christopher Brickell, Mitchell Beazley, London. Titles include *Pruning*, 1979, Simon and Schuster, New York, 1988; *Plant Propagation*, 1979, Simon and Schuster, New York, 1988; *Gardening Techniques*, 1981; *Lawns, Weeds and Ground Cover*, 1989; *Container Gardening*, 1990

Scott-James, Anne, *The Best Plants for Your Garden*, Conran Octopus, London, 1988; published as *Perfect Plants, Perfect Garden: 200 Most Rewarding Plants for Every Garden*, Summit Books, New York, 1988

Thomas, Graham Stuart, *Perennial Garden Plants*, 3rd edition, Dent, London, 1990

Thomas, Graham Stuart, *Plants for Ground Cover*, Dent, London, 1990

Page numbers in italics refer to captions and to the growth charts.

ACKNOWLEDGMENTS
The publishers wish to thank the
following organizations and
individuals for their kind
permission to reproduce their
photographs on the following
pages of this book:
Clive Nichols: front jacket
Sue Atkinson: 80, 164
A-Z Botanical Collection: 48-9
Eric Crichton: 8-9, 16, 23, 25, 50,
51, 52, 78, 82-3, 85, 99, 100, 102
bottom, 103, 124, 165, 166
The Garden Picture Library: Brian
Carter 81 / John Glover 7, 128 / J
S Sira 127 / Wolfram Sterling 24-5
/ Didier Willery 26 / Stephen
Wooster 6
Jerry Harpur: 98, 163, 182, 184,
185
Andrew Lawson: 162, 178, 179
top and bottom, 180, 181
Mitchell Beazley: Paul Barker 3, 4-
5, 10, 18, 19, 46, 125, 129, 166-7
Natural Science Photos: Adrian
Hoskins 27
Oxford Scientific Films: Patti
Murray 20 / Harry Taylor 21
Philippe Perdereau: 22
Photos Horticultural: 84-5
John N Walker: 47, 101, 102 top,
183
Wildlife Matters: 79

PICTURE RESEARCHER:
Christine Rista